Wired
STYLE

ALSO BY CONSTANCE HALE

Sin and Syntax: How to Craft Wickedly Effective Prose

Principles of English Usage in the Digital Age

Constance Hale & Jessie Scanlon

Broadway Books // New York

Broadway Books titles may be purchased for business or promotional use or for special sales. For information, please write to: Special Markets Department, Random House, Inc., 1540 Broadway, New York, NY 10036.

Visit our Web site at *www.broadwaybooks.com*

Library of Congress Cataloging-in-Publication Data Applied For

ISBN 0-7679-0372-2

FIRST EDITION

Designed by Pei Loi Koay

00 01 02 03 04 10 9 8 7 6 5 4

Contents

Acknowledgments

Many people helped imagine the 1996 version of *Wired Style*, worked on its sentences, and continue to inspire us in this new edition. Tops among them are Louis Rossetto, John Plunkett, Kevin Kelly, and John Battelle.

A new cast of characters, however, had a more direct hand in this upgrade. We cannot thank Paul Boutin enough. He lent us his high-density mind as well as his high-flying wit, and he scrutinized the manuscript from A to zine.

Paul Donald, Jesse Freund, <Jim> Jeffrey, Todd Lappin, Eugene Mosier, Steve G. Steinberg, Brad Wieners, and Michael Wise also lent us valuable braincycles. Our stick-to-itive researcher Julie Greenberg dug deep, while Anh-Minh Lee cast her searches far and wide.

Editors and honchos at various publications gave us pieces of their minds: especially John Battelle at *The Industry Standard*, James Glave at *Wired News*, and Scott Rosenberg at *Salon*. So did a few writers, including Chip Bayers, Paulina Borsook, Dan Brekke, Mark Frauenfelder, and Stephen Keating.

We are also indebted to two very special word nerds: Gareth Branwyn and Eric S. Raymond. Branwyn's Jargon Watch column in *Wired* (and his book of the same name) sparks many a laugh as it raises the bar for anyone writing about tech tongues. Eric S. Raymond is a human database of hacker culture—he has guided us in private emails, in his *New Hacker's Dictionary*, and in the Jargon File Version 4.1.2 he maintains at *www.ccil.org/jargon*.

Gigathanks go to Robert Cailliau, Vint Cerf, Danny Hillis, John McCarthy, Bob Metcalfe, Jef Raskin, Dennis Ritchie, Larry Roberts, and Ray Tomlinson. They generously ironed out some wrinkles in our account of the history of technology.

We fly many questions by a group of the best copy editors we know: Emily McManus and Steve Mollman at *Wired* magazine, Tony Long at *Wired News*, Merrill Gillaspie at HotWired, Glen Boisseau Becker at *PC Magazine*, Gina Preciado at ZDTV, Beverly Hanly at LookSmart, and Felicity O'Meara at Autodesk and other places.

Version *2.0* of *Wired Style* would have been vaporware had it not been for the support of Todd Sotkiewicz and Katrina Heron at *Wired* and the patience of our agent, Wendy Lipkind. Our editor, Susanne Oaks, never actually said, "Where the *hell* is the manuscript?" And we _thank_ her. Others at Broadway Books helped smooth the tracks for this tome, especially Lisa Olney, Rebecca Holland, David Coen, and Pei Loi Koay.

Constance Hale would also like to thank the first geek in her life, an engineer with a love of history and poetry who happens to be her dad: Joseph Ganahl.

Introduction

Writers today must navigate the shifting verbal currents of the post-Gutenberg era. When does jargon end and a new vernacular begin? Where's the line between neologism and hype? What's the language of the global village? How can we keep pace with technology without getting bogged down in buzzwords? Is it possible to write about machines without losing a sense of humanity and poetry?

Traditional style manuals tend to be starchy, and offer little help in writing fluently and colloquially in and about the digital world. *Wired Style* is intended to complement those guides by digging into questions that writers and editors confront daily—questions of style and substance that Chicago and AP (not to mention Strunk & White) don't even imagine.

You might call *Wired Style* an experiment in nonlinear, networked editing. When a new technical term, a bullshit buzzword, or an especially gnarly acronym hits our screens, we send emails to various editors and style divas. *Wired Style* is the result of these online discussions, which are guided by actual usage rather than rigid rules. When it comes to a choice between what's on the Web and what's in *Webster's*, we tend to go with the Web. Like new media, *Wired Style* is dynamic and rule-averse. (Beware: the digital dictions in this book will soon ache for updates and clarifications. Please feel free to ply us with questions by emailing *wiredstyle@wired.com*.)

This book reflects *Wired*'s fascination with science and technology and the lexicons evolving out of those worlds. We assume an informed and inquisitive audience—readers familiar with, or at least curious about, the esoterica of our subject. Our style is not to tell the techies of the world to eschew jargon and adopt *New Yorker* grammar; nor is it to force jargon on journalists content to dwell in analog subject areas. We *are* trying to convey the excitement of technological innovations—in the language of those who create them.

We don't dumb things down. We don't shrink from experimentation. And as we push the boundaries of language and form, we follow 10 principles. The first five relate to prose style—how to write well in an ever-changing mediascape of email, glossies, Web sites, and biz pages. The second five relate to copy-editing style—how to spell and punctuate the new terms barraging us daily. We hope these principles can guide you and give you a feel for the way language is evolving as we head into the next millennium.

PRINCIPLE 1: THE MEDIUM MATTERS

Are you posting? Emailing? Writing for the Web? Forget the age-old tradition of letters. Language today is being stretched by cables and condensed by monitors. Writing caroms from elegant pages to terse emails, from crude pagers to whiz-bang Web sites. In a world of scarce bandwidth, small screens, and ever-more media sources competing for our attention, every word and sentence must score a high signal-to-noise ratio. And because every context sets a different "signal," we need to craft our messages to suit the medium and its audience.

Let's start with email. Email is instantaneous. Email is free. Email is "tit-for-tat communication," writes Guy Kawasaki in *The Guy Kawasaki Computer Curmudgeon.* "You ask. I answer. You ask. I answer. You're not supposed to watch the sun set, listen to the surf pound the sun-bleached sand, and sip San Miguel beer as Paco dives for abalone while you craft your E-mail."

A cross between a conversation and a letter, email is as fast as a telegram and as cheap as a whisper. It is more artful than conversation: alone at your screen, you are able to reflect quietly and compose carefully. At the same time, you sense the presence of others and await their rapid, earnest responses. The impersonal computer screen seems to invite a no-holds-barred communication that is, paradoxically, intensely personal.

Think blunt bursts and sentence fragments. Writing that is on-the-fly—even frantic. Media critic Jon Katz calls it "a whole new fractured language—definitely not as elegant or polished as English used to be, but in a way, much more vital."

What makes email more vital? A well-written electronic missive gets to the point quickly, with evocative words, short grafs, and plenty of white space. Spelling and punctuation are loose and playful. (No one reads email with red pen in hand.)

Headings, or subject lines, play cleverly with words. (Think artful haiku.)

Now that email pops up on pagers or palmtops, it needs to be pithy. Motorola's ads for Skytel pagers epitomize the rough urgency of email, with a comic twist:

```
MARIE ANTOINETTE
PEASANTS ARE RESTLESS.
DO NOT MENTION  CAKE.
TRUST ME.

CAESAR KEEP YOUR
EYE ON BRUTUS
I LL EXPLAIN LATER.
```

Pith and punch also define posting on the Web, The Well, wherever. If email is an intimate conversation, posting is a dinner-party debate. Perform well and you can stay indefinitely; perform badly and you will be ignored—or even asked to leave. In a post, you must still avoid unnecessary verbiage while you stretch and preen. But whether you are posting to a chat on AOL or to a conference on The Well, your words must keep readers riveted.

"The Net has created this huge stage for people," says *Salon*'s Scott Rosenberg. "But it's like a stage at a county fair: it's a competitive market." In the best online forums, Rosenberg adds, writing becomes a kind of performance art—heightened in style and enlivened by the stage presence of the posters.

› › ›

Email, posting, and other less formal kinds of online writing have influenced the way publishers are reinventing writing on the Web. Designed to be so simple that anyone could use it to publish research—which could be viewed by anyone on any machine anywhere—the Web quickly spread beyond the science world. Today it's home to everything from deep databases to e-commerce to multimedia extravaganzas.

Web writing must keep the often warring elements of words, pictures, and code in exquisite tension, combining motion, depth, immediacy, interactivity, usability—and speed. Ideally, a Web page loads as fast as the eye can read.

Until we have brilliant, high-definition flat-panel displays, people won't turn to their screens for leisurely reading. Now more than ever, brevity is the soul of wit. Look to the Web not for embroidered prose, but for the sudden narrative, the dramatic story told in 150 words. Text must be complemented by clever interface design and clear graphics. Think brilliant ad copy, not long-form literature. Think pert, breezy pieces almost too ephemeral for print. Think turned-up volume—cut lines that are looser, grabbier, more tabloidy. Think distinctive voice or attitude. (More on that in the next principle).

"The slow windup is very hard to pull off," notes *Salon*'s Rosenberg. "You have to work to keep the reader *in* the story, *at* the site, *within* this activity—as opposed to conferencing or shopping—and *on* the computer."

If it's breaking news you're writing, the Web's the AP, all over again: *USA Today*–style summaries, ledes that pull you in fast, pyramids of information with sharp points. If a narrative needs space, jump it to an inside page, but break on a cliffhanger.

Or try snake text—one long, narrow, must-be-scrolled-but-easy-to-read-on-any-browser column on a white background. Writers for *Suck* pour their gleefully abusive attitude into the snaking form, with parodies like "Sex and the Single URL" on the tastes of technolibertarians. In it Justine (aka Paulina Borsook) doles out tips on how to "tease, please, and capture the heart of the right anarcho-capitalist":

Fashion tips:

DO wear your "This Shirt is a Munition" RSA T-shirt.

DON'T wear your "Solidarity Forever UPIU/AIW Local 837 Lock-Out" T-shirt.

Accessories/props:

DO have on your coffee table the original, green-cover edition of *Bionomics*; hardcover edition of *Out of Control*; *Crossing the Chasm*; photocopy of *True Names*; an original French-language issue of *Barbarella*; the Re/Search *Modern Primitives* issue; the *Economist* with your subscriber label discreetly visible; a 1985 issue of *Reason* (to show you are an early adopter); fund-raising appeal from the Progress and Freedom Foundation.

DON'T have on your coffee table *Savage Inequalities*; *Which Side Are You On*; *Resisting the Virtual Life*; *Why Things Bite Back*; *The New York Review of Books*; *Sierra*; *Z*; *Paris Review*; any novel that's not science fiction or a technothriller; fundraising appeal from the Silicon Valley Toxics Coalition.

To Suckster like Justine, hypertext links offer the chance for an extra dose of irony. For less jaded journalists, hypertext can be a delight—and it can also be a distraction. Links make sense in certain kinds of narrative. They give you footnotes sans paper cuts. But examine your hyperlinks carefully. Do they enrich the story? Do they build in background—the onscreen analog to a newspaper's info grafs and boxes? Check out the artful way links float in the margins of *Feed* and *Salon*, but don't publish a hypertext *Odyssey* that makes the reader's journey as arduous as a Greek hero's.

Remember also that the Web is about conversation. "This is the only media context in which your audience is sitting at a keyboard, ready and able to respond now," says *Salon*'s Rosenberg. "It's not just 'What is your voice as a writer and how effective a stylist are you?' You are not doing your job seriously if you are not including your email address in your byline or setting up a forum for discussion."

"If you don't integrate public feedback," agrees John Coates of the news site SF Gate, "you will lose credibility."

On the Web, you forget your audience at your peril—a scorching flame is only a click away. But the principle applies offline as well: media should connect the writer and the audience.

PRINCIPLE 2: PLAY WITH VOICE

In this era of "client/server databases," "vertical portals," and "high-bandwidth networks," we are awash in data. But good writing is not data. We turn to literary journalism not just for information but for context, culture, spirit, and color. We respond to voice. Not the clear-but-oh-so-conventional voice of Standard Written English. Not the data-drowned voice of computer trade journals. And not the puréed voice of the mainstream press. The voice of the quirky, individualist writer.

Voice captures the way people talk. Voice adds attitude and authenticity. Voice is the quality of writing that lets the reader know that a story is coming from *someone* who has been *somewhere*. Who but science fiction writer Bruce Sterling could go to Prague and send back an account whose every nanodetail is given in the drawl of a Texas cyberpunk?

> The desk I'm working on right now has a big container of little hard floppies, an even bigger container of big wobbly floppies, a bouquet of yellow flowers in a vase, two short-story collections, a voltage converter, a QuickTake camera, an emigré magazine, a thick, English-language monthly calendar of Prague cultural events, some Czech rock tapes, a joystick, a printer, a pack of Dunhills, and a rotary phone.
>
> The rotary phone here is truly a device from hell. This phone is an

> ancient Siemens pulse unit. Out the back of the set comes a yard of round-as-a-noodle, gray Czech phone wiring, which ends suddenly in a splay of four bare wires: white, brown, green, and yellow. The green and yellow wires end in severed copper stumps, while the white and brown wires enter a small plastic doohickey. From the other side of this makeshift gizmo comes a flat American phone wire, with four little internal wires of its own. This time, the black and yellow wires are dead stumps, and the red and green wires are the unhappy survivors. This butchered American phone wire runs 6 inches and ends in a modem, and I don't mean a modem with a label or a shell. I mean a bare piece of green circuit board with some Malaysian and Filipino bit-eating caterpillars and a naked little tin speaker. Yet another American-style pinch-clip phone cord exits from this inert modem and trails into a Czech domestic phone outlet, which is an alien doorknob-like object big enough to brain someone with. And out of the bottom of this ceramic phone outlet comes a truly ancient length of round, pre-Communist-era phone cord, running down the wall, along the baseboard, and behind a towering glass-fronted bookcase of Czech literary classics, to god-only-knows what eldritch, electromechanical, Nazi-era, phone-switch destination.

Sterling invents his own words when he needs them (Czech women are "Praguelodettes"), strings together lines of nouns when just one won't do ("Magor is the perfect model of a Czech hippie-dissident-tribal-shaman-poet-heavy dude"), and pulls no punches ("but he's not what you'd call commander-in-chief material"). And he throws *god* in there at just the right moments.

"As a lover of the plain simple straight-ahead commonsensical and above all *human* style of the master Jonathan Swift," says *The New Yorker*'s John Seabrook, who is a regular of both Echo and The Well, "I am so pleased to see citizens of the Net quietly keeping the fires of great prose alive." What does Seabrook find so appealing? The posts seem to have been "written on the spot, in one draft, immediately. 'Like Jack Kerouac without the benzedrine' as I once read Richard Preston saying."

"Writing with voice" might mean going for the unexpected, the rough-edged, the over-the-top. Resist filing it down, polishing it, editing it away. Look to the guidelines of The New Journalism, proposed by Tom Wolfe in 1973: "There are no sacerdotal rules; not yet in any case . . . if the journalist wants to shift from third-person point of view to first-person point of view in the same scene, or in and out of different characters' points of view, or even from the narrator's omniscient voice to someone else's stream of consciousness . . . he does it. For the gluttonous Goths there is still only the outlaw's rule regarding technique: take, use, improvise."

Celebrate subjectivity. Write with attitude. Play with voice.

PRINCIPLE 3: FLAUNT YOUR SUBCULTURAL LITERACY

Shared knowledge connects the writer and the reader. It forms a bridge from the type on the page (or the screen) to the deeper meanings and nuances of words. Social critic E. D. Hirsch, Jr., calls these connections "cultural literacy, the context of what we say and read."

Any literary endeavor must stoke the collective knowledge of its audience. Though new forms of broadcast like CNN are reaching larger audiences and making broadcast broader, most audiences are smaller, self-selected groups. Call them niches, elites, subcultures, or tribes—our contemporary world is crammed with these cliques, bursting with expertise and passion. You can find them in any field—programming, surfing, rocketry, civil rights; from them come new fads, new art, new goals, and new language.

These communities share collective memories, mores, literature, and language. *Wired*'s niche is the culture of technology; we write for a reader who shares not just an interest in but also a body of knowledge about the digital age—its time line and history and cast of characters. The digital age provides the context that gives our community its allusions, metaphors, and mythologies.

Consider your own context. Narrowcast. Talk to your audience. Speak the culture.

PRINCIPLE 4: TRANSCEND THE TECHNICAL

Jargon gets a bad rap among literary types. As a pejorative catchall for plain lack of eloquence, jargon is often equated with pretentious technical terms stuck where they don't belong, with highfalutin words calling attention to themselves when a single syllable would do, with strings of noun clusters and prepositional phrases that gum up a sentence like spilled Jolt on a keyboard.

But true jargon—the argot of a special trade or community—is lucid language and can be as elegant as it is meaningful. It's denotation: concrete, specific, direct, and necessary.

Writer Steve G. Steinberg must rely on jargon in his explorations of highly technical issues. He blends the technical with the typical—as in this example, where he explains one of the main problems of the World Wide Web: speed.

> Right now, even if you're using a fully stocked Pentium III and have a T-1 line running into your bedroom, the Web can seem overloaded and painfully slow. Conventional wisdom says the solution lies in new network technologies like ATM and fiber optics. But researchers are investigating how to change the way computers communicate to minimize pauses, stutters, and false starts. After all, using the Internet isn't just a matter of shouting, "Hey, wired.com, shoot me that GIF!" The Net has rigid protocols—or a stack of protocols, each relying on the one underneath—to define how to communicate.
>
> Protocol stacks make it easy to create new application protocols, since all the building blocks are provided. But building with prefabricated parts can be dangerous. . . . Too much time can be spent murmuring polite hellos and good-byes rather than transmitting data. This kind of handshaking, which exposes the latency of a network, is exactly what good protocols try to avoid. As network designers like to say, you can buy more bandwidth, but you can't change the speed of light.

Here the jargon is parsed out in just the right proportion to the clear prose. In too much writing, though, tech subjects are a swamp rather than a springboard, filled with useless gibberish (phrases like *nonzero-dispersion shifted fiber*) and overused words (marketing drivel like *ease of use*, *turnkey*, *utilization*, *interoperability*, and anything starting with *e-*, *cyber-*, *or techno-*).

When we hit paragraphs that begin, "By IP-multicasting over ADSL, ImagicTV can deliver programming over a carrier's multipoint network. Broadcasting several 3-Mbyte signals to each person . . ." we want to stop reading about technology altogether.

The best writers and editors mix the literary, the vernacular, and the precise. They get the geek lingua franca, but they lose the buzzwords and opaque alphabet soups. They use apposition and analogy to define tech terms, not esoteric technsplanations.

Writing with power and clarity about technology requires more than just spelling out acronyms, more than regurgitating PR talk. Grasp the technologies, then describe them with vivid language and clear metaphors.

PRINCIPLE 5: CAPTURE THE COLLOQUIAL

At *Wired*, we write geek and we write street. We insist on accuracy and literacy, but we celebrate the colloquial. Let writing reflect the vernacular of your reader, limning the lives and speech of the characters you describe.

Po Bronson does that when he captures—albeit tongue-in-cheek—the geekspeak of high-tech pundit George Gilder:

> Every time Gilder meets an engineer, they go through this sort of cascade of language syntax, negotiating like two modems, trying to find the most efficient level of conversation they can hold. It ends up sounding like the dueling banjo scene from *Deliverance:*
>
> **GEORGE:** "Hi, nice to meet you. Hey, that's a sweet access router over there. Wow, both Ethernet and asynchronous ports?"
>
> **STEVE:** "Yeah, check this baby out—the Ethernet port has AUI, BNC, and RJ-45 connectors."
>
> **GEORGE:** "So for packet filtering you went with TCP, UDP, and ICMP."
>
> **STEVE:** "Of course. To support dial-up SLIP and PPP."
>
> **GEORGE:** "Set user User_Name ifilter Filter_Name."
>
> **STEVE:** "Set filter s1.out 8 permit 192.9.200.2/32 0.0.0.0/0 tcp src eq 20."
>
> **GEORGE:** "00101101100010111001001110110000101010100011111001."
>
> **STEVE:** "..."
>
> **GEORGE:** "Really? Wait, you lost me there."

Digital culture has its own language and sublanguages: Usenet with its cancelbots and CancelBunnies, MUDs with their dungeons and wizards, online parlance with its BTWs, IMHOs, smileys, and rampant asterisks.

Sometimes, everyday slang gets converted into technical jargon (*bozo filters, kill files, mailbombs*). But "capturing the colloquial" can also work in the other direction: techie terms can become colloquial and take on a whole new life, as when the term for network capacity (*bandwidth*) becomes a metaphor for attention span (*I don't have the bandwidth to deal with that right now*).

In a profile of Tony Podesta, a colorful Washington lobbyist for high-powered high tech companies, writer Sara Miles notes that translation skills are essential to help geeks master the political nuances of Beltway squabbles over e-commerce and Internet telephony. Then she packs in a couple of quotes in which her subjects turn geek vernacular into metaphor:

> "Tony's a router," says the White House's Jeff Smith. "He knows how to get people from A to B." Or, as Podesta puts it, "I'm software. I'm a server, I'm a switch, I'm all of the above."

Write the way people talk. Don't insist on "standard" English. Use the vernacular, especially that of the world you're writing about. And avoid lowest-common-denominator editing: don't sanitize and don't homogenize.

PRINCIPLE 6: ANTICIPATE THE FUTURE

Language moves in one predictable direction: forward. Writers may often be guided by a certain nostalgia—reading the classics, looking up ancient etymologies, plumbing *The Oxford English Dictionary* for layers of meaning. And, sure, language reflects the richness of history. The phrase "brave new world" rolled from Shakespeare to Huxley, picking up steam along the way; it's now used frequently as a metaphor for the perils of the digital age. One of our pet verbs—*grok*—cropped up in Robert

A. Heinlein's *Stranger in a Strange Land,* reappeared in Tom Wolfe's *The Electric Kool-Aid Acid Test,* and has become a fixture in editorial meetings.

But technology is pushing us forward, toward the cultural and linguistic frontier. Techies invent terms daily; fresh slang sweeps through an online community within hours; new media shifts how we use words.

As technology writers, we must keep our eyes trained on the future. We must know the arc of language and strive to follow it. Faced with a dicey style question, we must try to anticipate the inevitable evolution of language, constantly asking ourselves: Where are style and usage headed? What's hype and what's here to stay? How does technology shape language?

The question is not *How has it been?* but *How will it be?*

Cyberspace was a mere figment of William Gibson's imagination in 1981 when he coined the word. Today it is on everyone's lips. So, we say, "Grow the language." Other neologisms we welcome happily include *digerati, netizen, gritch,* and *millionerd.*

"Save a keystroke" is another style commandment rooted in the way of the Net. As email and online writing continue to blossom, look for initial capital letters to slip into lowercase. Terms we've uncapped include *telnet, listserv,* and *webmaster.*

From computer commands like *whois* and onscreen nouns like *logon,* we have evolved this commandment: "When in doubt, close it up." Words spelled solid—like *startup* or *homepage* or *videogame*—may seem odd at first, but the now-common *modem* illustrates how quickly words move from the strange to the familiar: Who even knows that the piece of hardware allowing computers to talk to each other was once called a *modulator/demodulator?*

Our style for *electronic mail* is another example of the principle. *Wired* never used an uppercase *E* to abbreviate *electronic.* Sure, it's C-section, H-bomb, V-chip—but *E-mail* looked odd. (Few people online styled it that way.) As the Net caught on, and as more and more people started speaking in ASCII, the hyphen looked more and more anachronistic. "Hyphens ultimately vanish; words are concatenated; it's the way of the world," insisted Louis Rossetto back in 1996. "Electronic mail became e-mail became email. Yippee!"

So we spell *email* solid. The way of the Net is just not a hyphenated way.

That said, we write in English, not German. Words like *realtimevideostreaming* look downright Teutonic. Equally silly are polysyllabic words forced together as a brand. (Do *you* think RelevantKnowledge is better as one word?) But don't boycott solid spellings for simple words. When Webster's gives you a choice, close up compounds: *spinoff, diehard, hardcore.* We know from experience that new terms often start separated, then become hyphenated, and eventually end up as one word. Go there now.

PRINCIPLE 7: BE IRREVERENT

Provocative writing demands out-of-the-box thinking. In this age of interactivity, writers and editors should aim to elicit response. Know your audiences well enough to violate journalism's cardinal rules and to toy with conventions.

This might mean writing daring headlines—like "Nobody Fucks with the DMV," which got *Wired* banned from the racks of CompUSA. That headline not only captures the colloquial (it came from an editorial discussion of the story's focus) but it speaks the truth in the face of conventional wisdom.

Irreverence involves more than shock value. It's about giving a writer free rein to craft a story about VCs on Sand Hill Road that reads like nonfiction but is completely made up, like "The Relentless Pursuit of Connection," a satire of Silicon Valley by Po Bronson.

Conventional style manuals freeze the treatment of public institutions. But these organizations are an everyday part of our activities, our speech, our online existence. No one needs the tax man's name spelled out on first reference—*IRS* works fine. So does *FCC. The Department of Justice* and *DOJ* are equally acceptable; the name you use should reflect the writer's voice, not *Chicago,* 14th. Context can make *the spy agency* a perfectly acceptable replacement for *the NSA.*

The cardinal rules of so-called objective journalism would have us call the Senate's 1996 Exon Amendment (also known as the Communications Decency Act) "a provision that would prohibit the use of sexually explicit images or text over the Internet." We prefer to call a spade a spade. It was "censorship legislation."

We use the same rationale with major companies and celeb CEOs. When *The New York Times* runs a story on the man who turned software into a household word and amassed more money than God, it calls him "William H. Gates III, chairman of Microsoft Corporation." Most readers will recognize Bill Gates under any number of guises—including Mr. Bill, Chairman Bill, or bgates.

Likewise, why use the full corporate name of every company? Call Apple Computer, Inc. plain Apple. Call NETCOM On-Line Communication Services, Inc. just Netcom. Write like a person, not like *Hoover's Handbook of American Business.*

While we're on company names, let's tackle the quirky way tech outfits like to style their own names and products. *The New Hacker's Dictionary* pokes fun at the "BiCapitalization" and "studlycaps" seen in PostScript and PowerBook. According to the insidery handbook, "too many marketroids think this sort of thing is cute, even the 2,317th time they do it." We agree with the point, but we stick with company preferences as long as they aren't *too* out of line. Resist the urge to tame DirecTV, DreamWorks SKG, and Yahoo!, or to file down the idiosyncratic trademarks that reflect the habits of the computer industry. (But go ahead and avoid typographically ugly all-caps for long names and acronyms: Nynex, Lexis, Nasdaq, *USA Today*, Sega. When the company is pronounced as a series of letters, however, you're stuck: MSNBC.)

When we say "Be irreverent," we encourage you to do the following: Welcome inconsistency, especially in the interest of voice and cadence. Treat the institutions and players in your world with a dose of irreverence. Play with grammar and syntax. Appreciate unruliness.

PRINCIPLE 8: BRAVE THE NEW WORLD OF NEW MEDIA (OR, WHAT TO DO WITH—AARGH!—TITLES)

Digital technology has ushered in a new ecology of media. Lone PCs and scattered servers have spawned homepages, chat rooms, mailing lists, and e-zines. As the Macintosh and the Web have redefined publishing, CD-ROM adventures like *Myst* and networked games like *Doom* have redefined entertainment.

The boundaries between these media often blur. When works appear on paper, disk, or disc, or videotape—or in any combination of these—how are you to style titles and names? Start by focusing on the scope and scale of a piece rather than the medium. It's the *nature* of the creative work, not the platform, that determines how to style a title.

In the old days, a piece of writing became "published" when someone paid bucks to print it. Today, anyone can produce a homepage or start an e-zine. An online idea earns italics not just when it is creative, but when it passes both of two simple tests: Is it copyrightable expression? And does it have a wide audience? If it has the same number of viewers as a family photo album, don't treat it as a creative work. If, on the other hand, it *has* devoted readers or viewers, and if it *is* original content, it enters into the universe of italics.

In the world of new media, as in the world of old media, we need conventions—italics, quotation marks, capitalization—to separate discrete titles from the prose that surrounds them. Keep in mind, though, that styling titles is sometimes going to be different in print and online: if you are posting or publishing on the Web, your palette includes ASCII standards such as all caps, asterisks, or underscores as well as HTML tools such as color, underlining, and linking.

Here are our recommendations:

Traditional, and not so traditional, creative works

Treat the traditional arts, letters, and music in the manner of that analog bible, *The Chicago Manual of Style*. Books, newspapers, magazines and zines, television shows, radio shows, plays and performance art, visual arts, films—all are copyrighted, original content; all are italicized:

2600: The Hacker Quarterly [a zine)
Blade Runner [a film)
Fractal Fish [digital art)
Music for Airports [a musical recording)
The Nerve Bible [performance art)
The Raleigh News & Observer [a newspaper)
The Soul of a New Machine [a book)
Tech Nation . . . Americans & Technology [a radio show)
The X-Files [a television show)
Vibe [a magazine)

Creative works that are more limited in size or scope are set off not by italics but by quotation marks:

"My First Flame" [a *New Yorker* article by John Seabrook)
"As We May Think" [an *Atlantic Monthly* essay by Vannevar Bush)
"Johnny Mnemonic" [a short story by William Gibson)
"Do You Wanna Go Our Way???" [an MP3 masterpiece by Chuck D)

Newspapers and magazines are publishing on the Web as well as in print. Whether repurposed news or stories freshly reported for an online magazine, this is still copyrighted material, still intellectual property, still italicized:

Addicted to Noise [a rock rag)
CNN Interactive [CNN's online incarnation and search engine)
Electronic Telegraph [the world news from London)
geekgirl [a zine for and about grrrls in technology)
Playboy [a Web site boasting some 3 million pageviews a day)
Salon [an interactive art and culture mag)

Is a videogame a creative work? What about a CD-ROM version of the Yellow Pages? Remember, it's not the platform, it's the nature of the work that determines style. Just as we would italicize print copies of the *Encyclopaedia Britannica,* we italicize

Encyclopaedia Britannica Online, the Web edition of the big blue set. Microsoft's *Encarta* is a CD-ROM and a Web site—it doesn't even exist on paper. No matter: it's an encyclopedia, so it's italicized.

As for games, the days are over when all games were played with cards or on boards and styled in roman type. First came arcade games, like Pac-Man, that were played on coin-operated, self-contained machines—and for a while those titles were printed in roman type, too. Then came videogames, from the relatively simple *Mario Brothers* to the complex polygons of *Virtua Fighter*. Then came computer games like *Tetris*. Then the CD-ROM appeared, and with it games like *Myst* that were as much interactive fiction as anything.

Today, some games are released in all four digital forms. Titles that began as arcade games—like *Pac-Man* and *Mortal Kombat*—have become computer games. They may not be in Shakespeare's league, but italicize them anyway:

Asteroids [the quintessential '80s coin-op turned videogame)
Pong [the game that launched Atari and the industry)
Quake [the shoot-'em-up that doomed *Doom*)
SimCity [the original sim—a game of urban development)

Web sites

Whether individual homepages or constellations of separate pages accessed through one frontdoor, Web sites involve real-time interaction, HTML links, place-ness, and a sense of community. They are part publishing, part broadcasting, part narrowcasting, part casting for profits. They are dynamic, not static. Some are sleek, some sprawling, all are roman:

Awaken [get your Web sutras at *www.awaken.org/*)
CNET [Internet news service and TV network focused on tech)
ESPNET SportsZone [Web site of champions)
HotWired [articles, gonzo graphics, events, threaded discussions)
Justin's Links from the Underground [Justin Hall lives!)
sfgiants.com [news-cum-fan site, T-shirt store, and ticket office)
PeaceNet [network comprising BurmaNet and hundreds of mini-nets from around the world)

Online communities

Online communities are groups of netizens small enough to make up a social organism. A community might cluster in a computer conferencing system like Echo or in Usenet newsgroups like rec.music.gdead. A community might be made up of doctors, artists, investors, gays and lesbians, or elderly netizens who flock to bulletin boards or find each other in the public areas of online services like AOL and MSN. The names of online communities are styled roman and as proper nouns (except for Usenet newsgroups, which are styled all lowercase: alt.pets.barbecue). Retain the idiosyncratic punctuation and capitalization of the name:

GeoCities [millions of personal homepages grouped in neighborhoods of interest)

iVillage [the women's network, with channels ranging from finance to fitness)

Motley Fool [more than one million investors trading tips and strategies)

Online services

Internet service providers are commercial outfits in the business of getting you jacked in. They might offer a direct connection to the Internet via a dedicated line, or a dialup connection that lets you connect via a modem to a company with direct access. ISPs may also offer exclusive features, such as chat rooms and databases. ISPs are proper nouns, styled roman with initial caps.

America Online [the 18-million member club)

EarthLink [the "little ISP that could" is not so little anymore)

Portals are a front door to the Internet and the World Wide Web and offer a combination of community, email, news, travel services, shopping, and financial information. However irregular, they are not creative works, and so should be styled roman, retaining the company's spelling preferences:

Yahoo! [a catalog of URLs that became the king of portals)
Go2Net [a network of sites including Silicon Investor and MetaCrawler)
Deja.com [Usenet with an interface-lift and an e-commerce play)

Commercial databases offer information for a price. The names are spelled in all caps by the company, use initial caps only:

Lexis-Nexis [very extensive, very expensive legal and news library)
Dialog [science and technology resource owned by Knight-Ridder Information, Inc. and second only to the Library of Congress)

Search engines—conceived as the online incarnation of library card catalogs—are *supposed* to help you find stuff. They are trademarked names, not creative works.

AltaVista [Web scourer created by Digital Equipment Corp.)
Google [an innovative search-and-rank engine developed at Stanford University)
Inktomi [the engine of search sites such as Yahoo! and HotBot)

PRINCIPLE 9: GO GLOBAL

How can you be both local and global? Welcome to one of the central paradoxes of the digital age—and its style.

Stories of the global village celebrate cultures that blend indigenous character with global connections: Articles about Moscow's *tekhnari*, the scientists and engineers who launched dissident movements and shifted Russian culture. Or about a group of Hawaiian children in a schoolhouse in Pai'a, Maui, who use computers to chat in an ancient language with kids in New Zealand. Or about Star TV and BSkyB and CNN—international television companies whose news and entertainment businesses observe no borders.

It's a simple truth: today, no culture—or publication—is an island. The global village and the global economy are real.

Yes, we write in English, but in these Webbed times, writing from a US-centric perspective is hopelessly outdated. Anyone, anywhere, anytime can call up a Web site or visit a newsgroup, and the information must overcome a baffling kind of provincialism. This might require a simple style shift—ditching the foreign dateline rules of the Associated Press, for example. (Why can't Rio de Janeiro stand on its own? We all know it's in Brazil.) Or it might require rethinking how to present such mundane information as a phone number, a price, or a designated hour.

The time-honored tradition of avoiding foreign words comes off as leaden, even timid, in light of the Internet and the Web. The days of hot type are over. It's as easy to print italics as it is to print roman, so foreign words should be set off that way, whether the Hawaiian *lolouila* (computer, literally "electric brain"), the Japanese *keiretsu* (a cartel-like group of companies), or the Czech sídliště (workers' barracks). Word-processing programs and publishing software make it easy, so don't be lazy or xenophobic—take the time to figure out correct spellings and accent marks. And don't Americanize by, say, adding an *s* to pluralize a foreign word if that's not the convention in that language: "Japan's *zaibatsu* are responsible for 15 percent of Japan's gross national product." Similarly, don't slap an "Inc." or "Corporation" onto the name of a non-US company: it's probably plc (for Public Limited Company) in the UK; SA (for Société Anonyme) in France; AG (for Aktiengesellschaft) in Germany; KK (for Kabushiki Kaisha) or YK (for Yugen Kaisha) in Japan. These corporate suffixes may also help distinguish a US subsidiary or division from its foreign parent company.

Writing with a global perspective means being cosmopolitan: enjoying the best of other cultures and tongues, and resisting the impulse to put foreign ideas and phrases through a bottom-feeder filter. For specific pointers on following a globe-trotting style, see the entries on **currencies, measurements, phone numbers,** and **time zones** in the A to Z.

PRINCIPLE 10: PLAY WITH DOTS AND DASHES AND SLASHES (NOT TO MENTION !@#«$*)

When it comes to punctuation, the funnies have nothing over hackers. If you're writing on or about the Net, prepare for a clash of cultures—between copy editors and coders. The first live by the book, faithful to every mechanical rule; the second live by the keyboard, wildly appropriating every punctuation symbol in ASCII. Online, publishing meets programming—and punctuation leads a double life.

Take coding: the age-old markers don't merely punctuate sentences, they command them; #'s and !'s and /'s are the syntax of sentences in C++ and Unix. They are *as* important as letters, coequal members of the character set with which coders create. And though the symbols were borrowed from a printer's box years ago, they have taken on new meaning. The !, for instance, invokes a previous command (!3 would rerun the third command of that session history). Over the years, punctuation marks redefined by programmers were also renamed: a *tilde* (~) is a "squiggley," an *exclamation point* (!) is a "bang," a *number sign* (#) is a "hash," a "sharp," a "crunch," or a "crosshatch," and, according to the Jargon File (a compendium of all things hackish), the nicknames for *asterisk* (*) range from "star," "splat," "wildcard," and "dingle" to "spider," "aster," "times," "twinkle," and "Nathan Hale."

This shorthand is more than just wordplay; it allows programmers to speak a sequence of characters with very little ambiguity. If you want to tell another programmer to type "#!/usr/local/bin/perl," doesn't "hash bang slash user slash local slash bin slash perl" just roll off the tongue?

Today, these hacking terms have reentered the non-geek vernacular, springing from the technical back into the mainstream. Think of .com (or "dot com") and @ (the symbol of digital savvy). And consider Slashdot, which may be the only publication named for two punctuation marks.

Though computer scientists owned the bandwidth for decades, publishers eventually arrived to colonize the Net with standard punctuation. With missionary zeal, editors and copy editors have stayed faithful to print conventions, doing the best they can in the land of ASCII. Periods and commas are maintained, while book titles on the Web are differentiated with underscores instead of italics.

Meanwhile, the Net's posters and chatters have adopted a pidgin system that grafts traditional rules of punctuation with a willingness to break the rules in the service of free expression. Online writers have found new ways to convey the intonations of speech and the nuances of mood. In Usenet newsgroups, Web postings, and chat rooms, writes online scribe Robert Rossney, "people seem like lions pacing in a zoo: they're dying to break out of the cage that text-only discourse puts them in. The smileys, ASCII graphics, strange spelling, and acronyms that you see everywhere online are all ways of rushing at the bars."

Here's a classic ASCII-artist post from The Well:

```
Wavy Gumbo Ya (dooley)       Tue Jan 7 '86

Oh god! . . . I must be coming on . . . all my pixels have eyes and
my Hercules Card is squeezing GKS primitives out all over my
non-selectric keyboard and my sweaty hands.

        h  a  n  d  s  (they ve never looked like this)

   (I can see right through them to the goupy geometrics
melting on my keyboard)

<------S-P-L-A-A-T-T-------->>>>>>>>>>>>>>>>>| !15W01

Oh no! (fear pierced him) is this unixland? Where no halcyon,
DOSile breezes blow? Where all beer tastes like Henry s?
{{{{{{{{{{{{{{{{{{{{{{{{bum trip}}}}}}}}}}}}}}}}}}}}}}}}
So, what the hell . . . pass the nitrous tra la
set the controls for the heart of the sun ya a a a  a
                                                      a
                                                        a
 . . . . . and give me clouseau . . . .  @^0!0W501 STACK OVERLOAD
```

Other quirks common to the style of hackers have migrated into online writing. To Unix users, every shift key tells a story, and Unix denizens stubbornly retain case-sensitive Unix spellings—and thumb their noses at literary conventions. A username—*neanderthal*—would be kept down even if it starts a sentence. So would a command. This penchant for nonstandard styling bleeds over into tech company and product names. eBay can start a sentence; a paragraph can end on Yahoo!

Precision trumps traditional rules, says the Jargon File.

Inventions and innovations—whether in words or wiggles—"tend to carry very precise shades of meaning even when constructed to appear slangy and loose," according to the scribes at *www.ccil.org/jargon.*

Hacker habits persist, even in written docs, even when font changes and options like underlining and italics are possible. They include:

- Typing in ALL CAPS, a graphical user in-your-face that conveys shouting.
- Spacing an all-caps word or phrase L I K E T H I S, which makes your point loud *and* clear.
- Using untraditional characters to add stress or intonation. The asterisk is the star of emphasis in queries like "where the *hell* is the manuscript?"

  Other characters provide shades of meaning: "it's =late+. <gasp>." And "I want it ; \now/. Not /later/."

  An entire phrase can be emphasized—*the deadline was yesterday*—or each individual word, Mom-style: *the* *deadline* *was* *yesterday*.
- The underscore symbol also adds oomph, but is more frequently used for book titles: if you miss _one_ more deadline, _Wired Style_ is dead.
- Angle brackets, somewhat surprisingly, have become the MVPs of online punctuation, owing in part to their role in email (where they often enclose a sender's address) and in HTML (where they surround commands or tags). They are especially useful in email back-and-forths, because they offer a way to distinguish questions and replies:

```
In answer to your question
> but why, oh why, oh why
I can only say B E C A U S E. . . .
```

Then, of course, there are **smileys,** but for those we'll let you step into the A to Z.

The *A to Z*

Abilene Project

Named for an ambitious railroad established on the Kansas frontier during the 1860s, Abilene is a high-speed backbone and a testbed for advanced technologies such as multicasting.

Officially launched in April 1998 by the University Corporation for Advanced Internet Development, Abilene spans more than 10,000 miles, links 37 universities at 2.4 billion bps, and is 1,600 times faster than a T-1. See **Internet2.**

-able

The meaning of the suffix isn't so mysterious: "capable of being." It's the spelling of certain words that remains perplexing, especially tech neologisms and nouns ending in *e*: *clickable, downloadable, emailable, hackable, manageable, scalable, upgradable*. Use this rule of thumb: keep the *e* after a soft *c*, a soft *g*, and sometimes a *z*.

access

A noun indicating the ability to log on to the Internet or another network. Or the ability to plug in to the network of VCs with bucks to burn.

ACM

Founded in 1947, the **Association for Computing Machinery** is a major fraternity for computing professionals, the sponsor of innumerable conferences and workshops (the Special Interest Group or Sig- series, as in **Siggraph**), and the publisher of a widely respected newsletter.

The ACM is so prominent in cyberculture that science fiction writer Neal Stephenson even appropriated the name (if not the exact identity) in *Snow Crash:* "The dimensions of the Street are fixed by a protocol, hammered out by the computer-graphics ninja overlords of the Association for Computing Machinery's Global Multimedia Protocol Group."

Ada

Programming language used by the DOD and named after Lady Augusta Ada Byron King, Countess of Lovelace and daughter of Lord Byron. In 1843, at the age of 28, Ada developed the mathematical and theoretical designs for Charles Babbage's Analytical Engine (see **Difference Engine**), making her the mother of computer programming.

add-on

It began its life as an adjective but now also works as a noun (hyphen intact) for a piece of software or hardware designed to enhance the performance of another system. A synonym, when you're talking software, is **plug-in**.

AES

The **Advanced Encryption Standard** is the US government's next-generation, 128-bit crypto algorithm. In January 1999, the cryptocrats at NIST advised Uncle Sam to revise the current standard, noting that cracking **DES** has become increasingly more feasible given advances in technology. AES should hit the Net by January 1, 2002.

AFAIK

As far as I know—online, that is.

agent

Short for **autonomous agent**. Think of an agent as an entity that learns your preferences and then independently does things for you within a physical or virtual environment. It might be a robot, might be an auctionbot, might be a Web spider. It might retrieve info, filter incoming email, or recommend music.

Or it might just disappoint. Like artificial intelligence, agent technologies have yet to deliver the long promised digital Jeeves. See **bot**.

AI

For the full treatment, see **artificial intelligence**. The acronym is acceptable on first reference, and is often used as a noun—"an AI" is a thinking and nonbreathing thing.

algorithm

Named for the ninth-century Arab mathematician Al-Khowarizmi, the term denotes any system or method for solving a problem. These rhythms set the beat of the computer age.

alias

On a Mac, it's a pointer icon—usually kept on the desktop—that opens an application or file stored in another location. Unix geeks create aliases to replace long, bulky text commands.

alpha

An adjective—which sometimes stands alone as a noun—describing the precommercial, internal release of software or hardware. Then comes the **beta** release, which may be public. There is no gamma release—that's called the market.

alt.

Pronounced "alt-dot," this Usenet prefix refers to the for-fun newsgroups created freely by users: alt.zines, alt.aol.sucks, alt.culture.hawaii, alt.fan.drew_barrymore.

In colloquial contexts, "alt." has become shorthand for "alternative" and "hip." It can be used as a catchphrase independent of Usenet, as in the headline of a story about an online dispute—titled "alt.scientology.war."

Altair

The MITS Altair 8800 was the do-it-yourself computer kit that sparked the PC revolution. The machine, which graced the cover of *Popular Electronics* in January 1975, shipped on March 26 of that year with an 8080 CPU and a 256-byte RAM card. Its price—400 bucks. Its name—an homage to the *Star Trek* episode "A Voyage to Altair."

Among the lives changed by the Altair were those of Bill Gates and Paul Allen. "A major milestone for us," Gates has called discovering the box. "When we read the description of the Altair, we didn't know exactly how it would be used, but we were sure it would change us."

AltaVista

The geek's search engine. The Web tool created by Digital Equipment researchers in 1995 allows advanced queries in a complex command-line language. Since Compaq swallowed Digital and then sold off the engine to CMGI, AltaVista's geek cred has suffered: bottom-line constraints have forced the search tool to imitate its more consumerist competitors.

Alto

Developed in 1973 at Xerox PARC, the Alto was the first personal computer to use a graphical user interface and a mouse. The Alto was to Steve Jobs what the Altair was to Bill Gates.

Amazon.com

Launched by Jeff Bezos (pronounced "bay-zoce") in July 1995, the Seattle based online bookstore jump-started the engine of e-commerce, becoming *the* paradigm of online retailing. It also became a verb: *to amazon* is to make an end-run around an established company—Barnes & Noble, say—by offering its goods or services online at a lower cost.

America Online

The "You've Got Mail" company. In the spring of 1985, AOL was just a tiny startup called Quantum Computer Services, Inc. (Quantum's Qlink—the first BBS software with a graphical interface—allowed Commodore 64 owners to enter cyberspace.) CEO Steve Case, a young marketing specialist who developed his chops pushing hair conditioner and pizza, used America Online to bring the infobahn to Main Street, USA. Once derided as the "Carnival Cruise Lines of interactivity," AOL held its course. By the start of 1999, it was the world's leading online service, with 18 million subscribers—more eyeballs than the next largest 15 Internet service providers combined, according to market research firm IDC. In 1998, Case acquired onetime rival CompuServe and browser pioneer Netscape Communications.

analog

Not digital. It's more of a put-down than "anachronistic." As in, *She's so analog, she still carries a Filofax.* In the analog days, the word referred to a way to transmit or measure data in terms of continuously varying physical qualities—as with the shifting hands of a grandfather clock. See **digital**.

angels

Amateur venture capitalists and professional risk-takers who invest in Silicon Valley startups. Born on Broadway to refer to the sugar daddies of the stage, the slang term refers to the high tech world's new source of funding.

"So many engineers made a bundle in the '70s in hardware or in the '80s in software," writes Po Bronson, a chronicler of the Valley and its angels. "Plain ol' joes, now sitting on a wad of cash. The desire to be young again occurs at the same time they wonder, What am I going to do with all this money? Two problems, one solution: invest in startups. They're thinking one thing: endless youth. Here, take my wallet, take my bank account, build me a Web site that gives me a woody."

anonymity

A state of being in which you leave no electronic trace.

anonymous FTP

A procedure that lets you access a file server without entering an ID or password: type *anonymous* or *guest* in the userid field, any text string (traditionally your email address) as a password, and then transfer your file of choice. See **FTP** for more on **file transfer protocol**.

anonymous remailers

Servers (such as anon.penet.fi, run by Johan Helsingius in Finland until September 1996) that launder email, stripping out the sender's name, address, and other identifying info in the header. The technology has been incorporated into a new generation of **anonymizers**—Web-based services like the Anonymizer that combine strong encryption, pseudonyms, and proxy servers to let you browse the Web incognito.

ANSI

A privately funded federation, with both private and public members, pronounced "an-see." The oft-derided **American Na-**

tional Standards Institute is dedicated to promoting national (and international) technology standards.

AOL

The acronym is as recognizable as the online service provider's full name. In fact, the *AOL* in AOL Europe is *never* spelled out. The acronym has inspired variants like AOHell, All Outta Luck, and Army of Losers. Then there's AOLOL. See **America Online**.

API

You interact with your computer through the user interface. *Software* interacts with software through an **application program interface** such as JNI, the Java Native Interface through which any Java program can talk to any computer.

Apple

Formed in 1976 by Steve Jobs and Steve Wozniak in Jobs's parents' garage, Apple Computer, Inc. launched the personal computer revolution with the Apple II and made the mouse a household word with the introduction of the **Macintosh**, "the computer that changed everything." The introduction of the PowerBook—the first laptop to become a fetish—was followed by a streak of product bombs and dud CEOs. But Apple bore fruit again with the introduction of the iMac in 1998, and (after the return of marketing genie Steve Jobs) ranked seventh in worldwide PC sales in mid-1999.

application

Short for **application program** and often shortened to **app**. Think of WordPerfect, Photoshop, or PowerPoint.

Originally, the term referred to software programs that performed tasks for humans rather than tasks related to computer operations. That distinction has been blurred as Microsoft coded ever more functions right into the OS.

Don't mix apps and **applets**. The term for those small Java programs embedded in a Web page and designed to do specific tasks is not a synonym for "applications" in general.

Arpa

See **Darpa**.

Arpanet

The first wide-area network—and the precursor to the Internet—was built at **BBN** by the Advanced Research Projects Agency (**Arpa**) as a research-sharing tool. In 1969, the first four nodes were established at the University of California, Los Angeles; SRI International, in Menlo Park, California; the University of California at Santa Barbara; and the University of Utah. The first message was sent across the network from UCLA to SRI.

The Arpanet was eclipsed in the '80s by the National Science Foundation's high-speed NSFNet backbone and the regional networks connected to it. Around this time, people began to think of this collection of networks as an "internet." See **Darpa**, **NSF.**

artificial intelligence

Alan Turing conceived of computer intelligence in 1950; John McCarthy christened it "artificial intelligence" in 1955. AI pioneer Marvin Minsky once defined the controversial science as "trying to get computers to do things that would be considered intelligent if done by people."

AI researchers toiled in virtual anonymity for decades—until Mephisto. The relatively simple computer that checkmated Anatoly Karpov in 1990 seduced a skeptical public with visions of machines that think and learn as we do. Then came **Deep Blue,** which bested Garry Kasparov in 1997. The thousands of shopbots, chatterbots, and intelligent agents on the Web announce, less dramatically than Mephisto, the arrival of AI.

artificial life

The field applying biological principles to nonliving systems. It's part biology, part computer science, with engineering, robotics, mathematics, ecology, philosophy, and God knows how many other things thrown into the mix. Also **a-life**. Maverick researcher Chris Langton defined a-life as "the practice of synthetic biology." Writer Michael Schrage called it "the attempt to simulate all the essential traits of life—not just evolution—using silicon instead of carbon."

"As We May Think"

Published in *The Atlantic Monthly* in 1945, this essay by electrical engineer (and Manhattan Project veteran) Vannevar Bush described the first, albeit hypothetical, hypertext information system. He called it "memex," though we know it today as the Web:

> The human mind . . . operates by association. With one item in its grasp, it snaps instantly to the next that is suggested by the association of thoughts, in accordance with some intricate web of trails carried by the cells of the brain. It has other characteristics, of course; trails that are not frequently followed are prone to fade, items are not fully permanent, memory is transitory. Yet the speed of action, the intricacy of trails, the detail of mental pictures, is awe-inspiring beyond all else in nature. . . .
>
> Selection by association, rather than indexing, may yet be mechanized. . . . Consider a future device for individual use, which is a sort of mechanized private file and library. It needs a name, and, to coin one at random, "memex" will do. A memex is a device in which an individual stores all his books, records, and communications, and which is mechanized so that it may be consulted with exceeding speed and flexibility. It is an enlarged intimate supplement to his memory.

ASCII

Call it the electronic Esperanto: the **American Standard Code for Information Interchange** is the standard, unformatted 128-character set of letters and numbers that can be represented by a seven-digit binary number between 0000000 and 1111111. It includes the pipe (|), the tilde (~), and the backslash (\) but not italics, underlining, bold, *or* non-English diacriticals (ç, ñ, or é, for example). ASCII is being replaced by the **Unicode** standard, which includes Asian symbols and other foreign characters.

We leave this acronym, pronounced "ass-key," all uppercase in deference to its place in the keyboard universe.

ASP

Beware this acronym. It can be shorthand for **application service provider,** a company providing Net-based services to businesses—everything from maintaining an e-commerce site to handling payroll. But it can also stand for **active server page,** Microsoft's standard for dynamically generated Web pages.

asynchronous

An adjective describing an operation performed in the background, independent of other simultaneous processes. In communications, asynchronous messages can be transmitted at any time. Telephone communication is synchronous; voicemail is asynchronous.

asynchronous transfer mode

Also **ATM,** it bears no relation to a plastic bank card. This protocol offers a single standard for voice, video, and data, transmitting at up to 622 Mbps. As Steve G. Steinberg writes, "Think of ATM data transmission as a train carrying ATM cells. The cell trains depart from your phone or computer and are then routed to their destination by ATM switches, which act like a switching yard: trains arrive, cells are switched to the correct output line, and the newly formed trains are sent out."

Its teasing nickname "Another Terrible Mistake" reflects the fact that ATM is a hot-button issue in networking circles, where it's increasingly considered an unnecessary layer of the protocol stack.

@

This curvaceous little character and fixture in every email address has a long history, possibly originating as a medieval ligature or contraction of the Latin *ad* (meaning "to, toward, at"). In the 19th century, it was used in cursive, commercial handwriting, as in "3 apples @ 10 cents an apple," and it was eventually called the "commercial A" or the "commercial at" in English, French, Italian, and Russian. The Chinese, meanwhile, call it a "little mouse," Danes and Swedes an "elephant's trunk,"

Germans a "spider monkey," Italians a "snail." Israelis pronounce it "strudel," and Czechs say "rollmops."

In writing, use the @; in speech, call it the "at sign."

In email, the @ is the brainchild of Ray Tomlinson, an engineer at **BBN**, who sent the first network email one day in 1972. Tomlinson needed a character that didn't occur in names, so that a computer could easily distinguish between the recipient and the address. He looked down at his Model 33 Teletype keyboard, focusing on its dozen punctuation marks. "The @ seemed an obvious choice because I didn't know anyone with an @ in their name, and the character had the added meaning of being 'at' the institution," Tomlinson says. "The irony is that @ is now becoming part of the names of things."

Speaking of names—like @Home—don't translate the "@" to "at," a change that *could* cause confusion or error and *would* lose the digital connotations.

@Home

The Mountain View, California, service that's delivering Internet content into homes via cable modems. In a frenzy of convergence in early 1999, the company—sometimes styled At Home Corporation—merged with the portal Excite to become Excite@Home, though the future of the partnership is uncertain.

Note: @Home is still acceptable in reference to the service.

Atari

An American company founded by Nolan Bushnell, Atari dominated the videogame market during the early '80s but foundered in the Sega era of hi-res special-effects games. Although *Pong*, *Asteroids*, and other classic games have been given a second chance by the toy giant Hasbro (which purchased rights to the dead brand in 1998), the name Atari is still a warning to cocky new gaming companies.

ATM

See **asynchronous transfer mode**. The acronym is OK in context, but beware: ATM could also mean "automated teller machine" or "Adobe Type Manager."

AT&T

American Telegraph and Telephone, founded in 1885, settled into our consciousness as Ma Bell. In 1984, government trustbusters broke the company into seven local Baby Bells and one long-distance provider, which kept the name AT&T Corporation. (A second split in 1995 spun off Lucent and NCR Corporation.) The original breakup marked the beginning of the end for old-fashioned telecom monopolies and the first step toward truly global data networks. With 90 million customers, AT&T remains the largest long-distance service, and one intending to grow: in 1999, the company bought into cable through TCI and MediaOne, took over IBM's networking division, and began to work with Microsoft on broadband. See also **Baby Bells, RBOCs.**

attention economy

The Net marketplace, in which information is plentiful, attention is the scarce resource, and wealth is defined in terms of eyeballs.

Attention economics has been around for at least as long as commercial media, whose true wares are not sitcoms or magazines but eyeballs for advertisers. Attention economics helps explain the explosive growth of high-visibility navigation sites like Yahoo! and the proliferation of free (to the user) products and services.

authenticate

To verify the identity of a user or computer or person at the other end of a digital conversation. This verb is also used as a participle: **authenticated** Web sites require surfers to register their names, email addresses, and other identifying info before accessing. The related noun, **authentication,** refers to the technology that guarantees the recipient of an electronic message that the email came from a certain person, much in the same way a written signature indelibly identifies the sender.

avatar

In the offline world, the Sanskrit-derived word refers to the incarnation of a deity. Online, avatars are the incarnation of mere mortals, representations of ourselves through graphical handles or sometimes just text descriptions. The avatar—a cartoon, a collage of Marilyn Monroe photos, a fish—is essentially a placeholder, representing where you are in the virtual world.

In this digital context, the word avatar seems to have been coined twice: by Chip Morningstar and Randy Farmer for their online community Habitat, and by Neal Stephenson in *Snow Crash:* "Your avatar can look any way you want it to, up to the limitations of your equipment. If you're ugly, you can make your avatar beautiful. . . . You can look like a gorilla or a dragon or a giant talking penis in the Metaverse."

In the e-commerce world, your consumer profile and payment info are more valued than your persona. In the gaming world, however, avatars still rule.

Baby Bells

Sometimes referred to as **regional Bell operating companies** or **RBOCs**, the Baby Bells were created by the breakup of Ma Bell in 1984. The seven included US West, Pacific Telesis, Ameritech, Nynex, BellSouth, Bell Atlantic, and SBC Communications. Merger mania has shrunk that number: Bell Atlantic swallowed Nynex, US West is merging with Qwest, and SBC reached the Pacific and is close to owning Ameritech.

Baby Bills

The companies that would be created if the Justice Department were to split up the Microsoft empire. In an earlier era, the term referred to the wave of high tech startups (and their starter-uppers) around Seattle.

backbone

The main conduit of a computer network, to which all other users and networks connect. The Arpanet, and later the NSFNet, once served as backbones to the Internet. There are only a handful of major backbones today, and the top two—MCI WorldCom and SprintLink—handle close to 75 percent of Internet traffic.

backdoor

A nonstandard or secret way to access a system or application, built in by the designer. Why one word? Because you'd take the backdoor into a system and the back door into a programmer's house.

Also called a **trapdoor**. The **frontdoor** is the standard method you use to log on.

background

An adjective (as in *background printing*) that signals the multitasking ways of your computer, which can perform any number of operations (such as checking email or backing up files) while you wordsmith in Word.

Also a noun: the virtual staging area, behind the active window of a screen, in which those operations are performed automatically.

Used colloquially as a verb, the term means "to put on the back burner" as in: *Let's background the redesign until after the IPO.*

back up

To duplicate data for storage purposes. The verb must be separated from the preposition to allow for different conjugations like *backing up* and *backed up.*

backup

The noun refers to what you created (*I lost my only backup*) or to assistance or help (*Give me some backup*). The adjective, too, is closed up: *backup disk.*

backward compatibility

A nice concept—the idea that, say, your new computer will still run your old programs. But it's often ruined in practice by the high tech industry's predilection for **planned obsolescence** (i.e., designing stuff that requires consumers to upgrade their software and systems every year).

bandwidth

The capacity of a network to carry data, usually expressed in bits per second (bps). Bandwidth is also an internal computer issue, as in the speed at which a processor can talk to memory.

More figuratively, *bandwidth* refers to a person's mental resources or capacity to handle a workload: *He's high-bandwidth* or *That company has a bandwidth problem—nothing ever gets done.* Related terms include **high bandwidth**, a faster-than-whatever-you-got, fatter-pipe network (which today means DSL, T-1, or cable modem), and the buzzword **unlimited bandwidth**, that metaphysical, metaphorical absence of constraints dreamed of by all cyberphiles.

bandwidth hog

Anything that requires a lot of capacity. Can refer to people—online activists, say, who use the medium like a megaphone—or to greedy apps such as graphics files and videostreaming.

bang

Unix slang for "exclamation point." Programmers have come up with innumerable ways to talk code without stalling out on the polysyllables of punctuation. (See page 22.) Other synonyms for bang, according to the Jargon File, include *pling, excl, shriek, factorial, smash, cuss, boing, yell, wow, hey, wham, eureka,* and *soldier. Sharp* is one of the preferred nicknames for "number sign." Put 'em together and you get *shebang* (#!).

banner

Short for "banner ad," these interactive billboards on the Web were born along with HotWired, in October 1994. Blame them for interminable download times. Smaller thumbnail ads predated the banner but did not include links to an advertiser's site. Banner ads employing animation and other enhancements are termed **rich media**.

barcode

The conventional barcode—a patch of vertical black stripes of varying widths—is the icon of the information age, but new versions employ circular figures, dots, and two-dimensional patterns rather than bars.

The barcode has also taken on connotations of Big Brother, evolving from a supermarket tool (used to track inventory and reduce cashiers' errors) to a super marketing tool (used to track your spending habits and build a consumer profile).

Basic

Beginner's All-purpose Symbolic Instruction Code is a simple, though limited, programming language developed in 1963 at Dartmouth College by John G. Kemeny and Thomas E. Kurtz. Resist the temptation to write BASIC: this name is pronounced as a word, not a series of letters, so use an initial cap.

The first version of Basic for microcomputers was written by Bill Gates and Paul Allen in 1975. Microsoft Basic spread widely, and its reincarnations—**Visual Basic** and the Web's VBScript—dominate Windows app development, even if they bear little resemblance to the original language.

baud

A speed of data transmission, pronounced "bod." Named after the French scientist J. M. Emile Baudot (1845–1903), *baud* initially referred to a unit of telegraph signaling-speed—one Morse-code dot per second. In the dawn of modems, one pulse equaled 1 bit, so 300 baud was the same as 300 bps. However, modern higher-speed modems pump more than 1 bit per pulse, so the terms are no longer interchangeable. Today, modems measured in baud are relics.

BBN

Arpa may have designed the Arpanet, but **Bolt, Beranek and Newman Corp.** built it. The Cambridge, Massachusetts, company connected the first four nodes in 1969, and still runs a major Internet backbone. BBN was renamed GTE Internetworking after it was bought by the long-distance giant in 1997.

BBS

The first **bulletin board system** was designed in 1978 by Ward Christensen and Randy Suess. Similar systems soon appeared, offering email, public forums, files, and sometimes real-time chat. But the golden age of BBS culture, the late '80s, is over; the baud-rate, dial-in era has been eclipsed by high-speed, multimedia online options.

For those **BBSers** still stuck on the digital bulletin board, the plural is **BBSes**.

Bell Labs

The legendary AT&T Bell Laboratories, in Murray Hill, New Jersey, was once the richest and largest private communications lab in the world. Formed in 1925, Bell Labs gave meaning to namesake Alexander Graham Bell's dictum "Leave the beaten path and dive into the woods." The lab's scientific fraternity represents a veritable Who's Who of international research: William Shockley, Walter Brattain, and John Bardeen invented the transistor in 1947; Arno Penzias and Robert Wilson confirmed the big bang theory in 1965; and Dennis Ritchie and Ken Thompson developed Unix in 1969.

In October 1996, Bell Labs split into the AT&T Laboratories Research Division (owned by the long-distance company) and Lucent Technologies Bell Labs Innovations (today owned by Lucent).

beta

A public precommercial release of hardware or software, widely distributed to uncover bugs and glitches. Usage: *Download the beta at your own risk* or *The game is just outta beta.* See **alpha**.

Betamax

Proof that superior technology does not a successful product make. In the mid-1980s, the industry squabble over videotape and VCR formats—cheapo VHS versus the better Betamax—slowed the growth of the market and angered consumers. VHS became the standard, Betamax the specter.

binary

The essential adjective of the 0 or 1, on or off, black or white world of computing. A binary or **base-two number system** represents data in 0s and 1s. A **binary file**, with its information recorded in numbers, is unreadable by humans.

Why do computers use a base-two system? People settled on the decimal system, with its perfect 10, because we have 10 fingers and 10 toes. Computers, however, are electrical machines, and recognize only the existence or nonexistence of electric current. Charge, no charge. One, zero.

biometric

An adjective describing security technologies that measure and identify biological traits such as fingerprints or voice patterns. Biometric systems use the body as a password. Think of an ATM that scans your iris rather than reading your PIN. In the biometric future, more than beauty is in the eye of the beholder.

bionomics

The study of economies as ecosystems, not machines. Advanced by the Bionomics Institute, in San Rafael, California, the core idea of bionomics is that individuals, companies, and markets exist in a complex, adaptive web, in which technological advance is analogous to biological evolution.

bitloss

The loss of bits, or data, from a transmission. Also used colloquially to mean loss of memory, information, or important fine points. **Bitrot** is bitloss caused by a decaying storage medium rather than by faulty transmission.

bits and **bytes**

While it takes 8 bits—each designated either a 1 or a 0—to make up a byte (enough to represent a single letter, a digit, or a punctuation mark), *bit* is generally used to describe transmission speeds; *byte* is used to describe storage capacity. Bits and bytes are so small that for today's data-driven world big modifiers are required: Kbit (kilobit) and Kbyte (kilobyte); Gbit (gigabit) and Gbyte (gigabyte). Nevertheless, the bit still commands respect: coders refer to the most important function of a program as the **highest-order bit**.

According to *The New Hacker's Dictionary*, *bit* was coined in 1949 by computer scientist John Tukey during a lunchtime discussion of "binary digits." *Byte*, on the other hand, entered the lexicon at IBM in 1956 and came to equal 8 bits—the unit of memory or data necessary to store one ASCII character.

bitstorm

A network problem, such as a broken Ethernet card misdirecting packets at top speed.

bitstream

Flow of data over a network connection. Transmission of bits.

blackholing

An anti-spam tactic whereby a network or ISP automatically deletes mail from a certain domain.

bookmark

Netscape Navigator's digital dog-ear offers easy access to a favorite Web site. A list of bookmarks is sometimes called a "hotlist"; Microsoft Explorer prefers "favorites."

Go ahead, use it as a verb: *Bookmark my site, I beg you.* Think of *earmark* and *pockmark*, which also do double duty as nouns and verbs.

Boolean

Honored by many a Web search, George Boole is the 19th-century English mathematician who conceived a system that reduces sentences (*Dick is here and Edie is here*, or *Dick is here or Edie is here*) to algebra ($D \times E$, or $D + E$). Boolean logic—based on the case-sensitive operators AND, OR, and NOT—serves as the basis of machine intelligence and, hence, computer searches. A search for "love OR marriage," for instance, would retrieve documents containing either term independently, while a search for "love AND marriage" would produce a fairy tale.

boot

A verb, derived from **bootstrap**, as in *pull yourself up by the bootstraps.* A computer boots up or loads its system software when it is turned on. **Reboot** refers to restarting a computer and yielded the Unix-world maxim: "When in doubt, reboot."

Borg

The Cyborg invaders from *Star Trek: The Next Generation*. Their goal: to absorb all other races. Their catchphrase: "Resistance is futile. You will be assimilated." Their relevance: the Borg is used by geeks as a metaphor for Microsoft.

bot

Derived from **robot** and **knowbot** and spelled without an apostrophe, a bot is an artificial intelligence program, an alter ego, a digital workhorse. A bot is guided by algorithmic rules of behavior—*if this happens, do that; if that happens, do this.*

The word pops up everywhere, flung around to describe any kind of task-performing function, whether logon script, spellchecker, or digital butler. ("While the master or mistress is brewing coffee," writes Andrew Leonard, "the bot is off retrieving Web documents, exploring a MUD, or combatting Usenet spam.") Look for cancelbots, chatterbots, softbots, mailbots, warbots, hackbots, spybots, slothbots, and even autobid bots—the snipers of online auctions.

bounce

The "return to sender" of the Net. When an address is wrong or a mail server is buggy, an email will bounce back marked Undeliverable by the postmaster.

bozo filter

A program, which originated on The Well, that filters email from or postings by individuals on your b-list (**bozo list**). In Usenet, a **kill file** performs that same function.

bps

This measurement of the speed at which data is transferred (in **bits per second**) is the mph of the Internet. Variants include Kbps and Mbps.

Note: bps is not a synonym for **baud**.

Brave New World

The title of this 1932 science fiction book by Aldous Huxley borrows from Shakespeare's *The Tempest* ("O brave new world/That has such people in't!"). The phrase has been seized upon as a metaphor for a society in which technology and social engineering are used to force people to be happy. The slightest suggestion of a national identification card, for example, generates cries of a brave new world of government intrusion.

Increasingly, we're seeing writers borrow the words *brave new* and substitute *world* with a noun suitable to the specific context: *Do smart badges that track a worker's location in the office just represent a brave new workplace?*

A caveat: Don't let yourself water these potent words down to a wordy alternative to *new.*

brick-and-mortar

A retronym made necessary by e-commerce. The adjective specifies a store located on a street, with walls, a door, and a cash register that you walk up to.

The related term **click-and-mortar** describes an integrated e-commerce strategy in which Web commerce promotes traditional offline sales and services, and vice versa.

British Telecom

Globalization has made BT—Britain's answer to AT&T—a major player in telecom issues around the globe. British Telecommunications, as it's formally called, *almost* won the bidding for MCI.

broadband

An adjective that comes from the telephone world, where it refers to wider bandwidth than a standard phone line. In the popular press, broadband is a synonym for **high bandwidth.**

Less literally, the term is becoming a catchall—a way of compressing "the future of infinite bandwidth" into one word.

browser

These days, the term browser—which predates the Web—most often refers to the software you need to travel that world. In addition to speaking HTTP, the modern browser serves as radio, video player, electronic wallet, and security system. (Brand names include Netscape Navigator, Microsoft Internet Explorer, NeoPlanet, Lynx, and Opera.)

The **browser wars**—a cliché for the fierce battles between Netscape and Microsoft—animated the Justice Department's 1998 antitrust suit against Microsoft.

BTW

Online shorthand for **by the way**, used by netizens to preface chat ruminations. Lazy typists may use lowercase letters, but we prefer the caps.

bug

An error in the source code of a software program, often extended to mean any type of glitch. Euphemisms for the fuckup include "issue" and "undocumented feature."

Tech trivia buffs love recounting an etymology that includes the apocryphal story of naval officer, Harvard scientist, and Cobol inventor Grace Hopper, who discovered that a moth stuck in her Mark II had fouled her computer. But, alas, Grace didn't coin *bug*.

Related words include **debug, bug fix,** and **bug bash**—the coders' equivalent of a witch-hunt.

bundle

The high tech term for a "package deal." Take Microsoft Office, a bundled software product that includes a word-processing program, a spreadsheet, a database, and a presentation tool—products also sold separately. Software **bundling** gives consumers the option of buying a set menu or à la carte, whereas software **tying** limits consumers to the set menu.

Burning Man

A Woodstock of the '90s that has become an annual gathering of tribes: *Whole Earth* veterans, Silicon Valley techies, Bay Area ravers. Thousands of revelers, days of camping, dancing, mud bathing, nudity, and environmental art. The culmination of this Labor Day fest in Nevada's Black Rock Desert is the torching of a 40-foot-tall latticework wooden figure packed with explosives.

bus

This generic term denotes a computer data path on an integrated circuit, inside the CPU, between peripherals, or over a network. Examples include FireWire, PCI bus, USB, and the venerable **SCSI**.

byte

See **bits** and **bytes**.

C

More common than Basic. Crafted by Dennis Ritchie at Bell Labs in 1972, C is the programming language of almost all the software running on the Net. It dominates advanced applications programming. Traditionally, if you can't C, you can't hack.

C++

Developed by Bjarne Stroustrup, this adds object-oriented features to C.

"C makes it easy to shoot yourself in the foot," says Stroustrup. "C++ makes it harder, but when you do, it blows away your whole leg."

cable

Wire that dwarfs the capacity of copper. Installed originally to deliver cable TV, cable is often used colloquially as a synonym for that service.

The first cable networks appeared in 1948, providing TV service in areas unreachable by broadcast signals. In the early 1970s, policy changes and advances in satellite communications helped establish cable as a mass media, and in 1972 Sterling Manhattan Cable launched the nation's first pay-TV network, HBO.

Today, more than 90 million cable households can surf more

than 170 national networks. Cable services will soon include Net access, telephone service, and more.

Don't hyphenate the compound modifier: *cable TV titan*, *cable TV addict*.

cable modem

Technology that leaves your 56K in the dust. The hopes of many cable companies (not to mention AT&T) are riding on this device, which transmits digital information at (theoretically) up to 5 Mbps.

As *New York Times* reporter Peter Lewis put it, "a cable modem is related to a regular computer modem the way the movie *Speed* is related to *Driving Miss Daisy*."

cache

Small, fast memory that stores frequently used or recently accessed data. Pronounced "cash," derived from the French *cacher*, "to hide." Web engineers have focused on **caching** as a way to speed up the network. But this doesn't help when Web sites change frequently—the cached version is out of date.

CAD

Pronounced "cad," this acronym for **computer-aided design** can also mean **computer-assisted design**. Although AutoCAD is a trademarked program, made by Autodesk in San Rafael, California, CAD refers to any computer-enabled method of design.

caller ID

The ESP telephone feature that knows the name or phone number of the party at the other end of a ringing phone. Though caller ID may be controversial, it's not trademarked, so go with the lowercase spelling.

cancel command

A built-in option of most Usenet software. A cancel-command message you send out propagates around Usenet, server by server, looking for your original post to cancel it. Although not easy, it's possible to hack the cancel command so that it will erase other users' posts.

Canter & Siegel

In 1994, opportunist lawyers Laurence Canter and Martha Siegel spammed newsgroups with advertisements for their services. Outraged by this first commercial use of Usenet, netizens flamed back, overloading Canter & Siegel's email account and warning other Net marketeers. If Usenetters won this battle against aggressive self-promotion online, netizens in general are still fighting the war. For their part, Canter and Siegel went on to write *How to Make a Fortune on the Information Superhighway*. See **spam**.

-casting

This increasingly common suffix tends to indicate methods of disseminating information: **broadcasting** (the model for standard TV service and the Web), **narrowcasting** (catering to small demographic groups, analogous to niche marketing or cable television), **multicasting** (a bandwidth-saving trick of transmitting data once to multiple people rather than sending individual copies), **pointcasting** (live, online programming distributed to one person or machine), **simulcasting** (broadcasting programming over two separate channels or media at the same time), and **datacasting** (a digital TV term for transmitting stock quotes and whatnot along with the basic sound and images). Only time and bandwidth will tell if **netcasting** (live, online programming for a discrete audience) will stick as a term and a technology.

"The Cathedral and the Bazaar"

This 1998 essay by Eric S. Raymond, the renowned hacker and open source evangelist, galvanized the industry. Moved by the self-published manifesto, Netscape released source code for its Navigator browser.

In the metaphor, the "cathedral" represents the traditional mode of top-secret, proprietary software development, while the "bazaar" suggests a community of developers in which any coder contributes and the best code wins.

CC

A vestige of the days of secretaries and mimeograph machines, the abbreviation for **carbon copy** can be either a noun or a verb (whose past participle is styled **CC'd** and whose gerund is **CCing**). In email, a CC is a duplicate message sent to recipients in addition to the primary one. Unlike a **BCC** (blind carbon copy), a CC is recorded in the header (and so is not considered a blatant breach of netiquette).

CD

The **compact disc** was developed by Sony and Philips Electronics in 1982 and originally called a "digital audio compact disk." These silvery platters first outsold black vinyl in 1986. A number of related storage discs have cropped up to join the audio version: the CD-ROM (CD–read-only memory) differs from audio CD mainly in the hardware needed to read it. **CD-R** (CD–recordable) is also known as a **CD-WO** (CD–write once), as opposed to **CD-RW** (CD–rewritable). **CD-plus** and **enhanced CD** were outpaced by **CD Extra**, a format playable on audio CD players as well as PC multimedia CD-ROM players. **CD-I** (CD–interactive) combines not only audio, video, and text but also animation and special effects.

All acronyms are acceptable on first reference, but we caution against the increasingly common practice of calling CD-ROMs just "CDs," as the latter term could technically refer to most of the above.

cd:

The DOS command for **change directory** is the turn signal of the pre-Windows world.

CDA

Also called the Exon Amendment in recognition of its author, retired Nebraska Senator James Exon, the **Communications Decency Act** passed on February 8, 1996—aka Black Thursday—as one measure of a sweeping telecom reform bill. The CDA made it a federal crime to send a communication that is "obscene, lewd, lascivious, filthy, or indecent, with intent to annoy, abuse, threaten, or harass another person."

Positioned as a measure to protect minors from pornography, the bill was viewed as a direct attack on free speech online. It marked the political coming of age of netizens, who formed a strong and united opposition. The Supreme Court ruled the CDA unconstitutional on June 26, 1997.

CDA II, aka **COPA** or the **Child Online Protection Act** of 1998, is nearly identical to its predecessor. Struck down by a federal judge in February 1999, COPA is fighting its way through the judicial system.

CDMA

A spread-spectrum cell-phone technology that offers 10 to 20 times the capacity of analog networks and, according to its fans, audio quality and coverage superior to its rival TDMA. Pioneered and patented by Qualcomm, **code-division multiple access** transmits encoded bits of voice data, from multiple conversations, across a single frequency. The receiving **codec** reassembles the coded bits into a brilliant conversation.

Both CDMA and TDMA are more philosophies than protocols, making strict technical definitions impossible—there are close to a dozen CDMA standards around the world. No matter which network technology you favor, don't fear the acronym—"CDMA, a cellular network on steroids" tells a lay reader far more than "code division multiple access." See **cell phone, GSM, TDMA, wireless.**

CD-ROM

A silver disc able to store the equivalent of 1,500 floppies, the technology never lived up to its hype. Producers lived in a kind of *Field of Dreams* fantasy, believing that if they installed enough CD-ROM drives, people would come. The remains of Voyager—once the leading CD-ROM company were sold to Learn Technologies in 1997, signaling the end of the fantasy and, in many ways, the victory of the Web as the mass medium of interactive publishing. However, CD-ROMs (the acronym stands for **compact disc–read-only memory**) are still popular for software, videogames, and many educational and reference materials.

cel

A transparent sheet of celluloid (whence the name), a cel is an animation frame and the canvas of classic animators. Mickey Mouse, Donald Duck, Bugs Bunny—all sprang from celluloid.

cell

A word of multi meanings, a cell is a box of data in a spreadsheet program, a fixed-size packet of data in the communications world, and the geographic area covered by a single transmitter of a cellular network.

cell phone

Accepted shortening of **cellular phone**. Although a cell phone is a type of mobile calling device, not all long-range roaming phones are cellular: a cellular system works by passing the signal from one local transceiver to the next as the conversation travels across cells. Non-cellular mobile networks use one megatransmitter to blast the signal across the entire service area.

CERN

The **Conseil Européen pour la Recherche Nucléaire**, or the European Laboratory for Particle Physics, is known globally as CERN. The Geneva lab is also known as the 1989 birthplace of the Web.

CES

The winter Consumer Electronics Show in Las Vegas, first organized in 1967, spawned a series of gadget orgies, all sponsored by the Electronic Industries Association (which sometimes calls itself the Electronic Industries Alliance).

Douglas Coupland went to CES, and this is what he found: "Thousands of men, for the most part, wearing wool suits with badges saying things like: Doug Duncan, Product Developer, MATTEL. . . . Everyone loads up on free promo merchandise like software samplers, buttons, mugs, pin, and water bottles as they dash from meeting to meeting. The booths are all staffed by thousands of those guys in high school who were good-looking but who got C pluses; they're stereo salesmen now and have to suck up to the nerds they tormented in high school."

CGI

Watch the context. To Hollywood networkers, the acronym means **computer-generated image**: the *Titanic* you watched sink, or the toys in that CG success, *Toy Story*.

To computer networkers, CGI means **common gateway interface**, a communication standard that defines the rules of conversation between a Web server and other software on the same computer. The app that processes an online order form and emails you a confirmation is often a CGI program.

CHA

What every Web site strives for. Short for **click here asshole** and pronounced "chaw," **CHA** is the ability to draw an audience. What makes good CHA? Web producers and advertisers are still chewing the question.

chaos theory

The study of complex, self-organizing systems, both natural and social, ranging from traffic jams to the stock market. Also known as the science of complexity, chaos theory is concerned with the patterns and regularities that create order out of disorder.

chat

The real-time banter of the online world. Don't dismiss the phenom for its often less-than-inspiring content; **chat rooms** made AOL into a $3 billion company.

chip

Short for **microchip,** one of these babies contains thousands of microscopic circuits etched in tiny silicon wafers. The microchip is the brain of the computer, allowing it to think (using **logic chips** or **microprocessors**) and remember (thanks to memory or **RAM chips**). Chips control everything from processing speed to the monitor display.

The technology has two independent inventors: Jack Kilby built a germanium chip at Texas Instruments in 1958, and Robert Noyce announced Fairchild Semiconductor Corporation's silicon version in 1959; a decade of legal battles ensued. In 1968, Noyce founded Intel, where a young engineer named Marcian E. Hoff Jr. built the first microprocessor, the Intel 4004.

Related terms include **chip architecture**, **chip fab**, **chipmaker**, and **chipset.**

churn rate

Employee turnover. Customer disloyalty. The rate, for instance, at which people sign up for AT&T's new long-distance package only to abandon the service for MCI's latest better offer.

circuit switching

The technology of Ma Bell. You pick up the phone, dial a number, and the line is yours for as long as you want it. That continuous connection, that channel, is as dedicated as your one-and-only.

Circuit-switching, however, is gradually, grudgingly, losing out to the more efficient **packet-switching** technologies of the Internet.

CISC versus **RISC**

CISC ("sisk") chips—such as Intel's Pentium—were designed to process several low-level operations or calculations in each instruction. RISC ("risk") processors were designed to execute instructions more efficiently than the preexisting CISC architecture.

CISC won the battle of the processors—but only by copying its competitors' ideas, say onlookers. We let bygones be bygones. And we don't spell out **complex instruction set computer** or **reduced instruction set computer.**

Cisco

Think of this networking equipment giant as the plumbing company of the Internet.

Cisco Systems (named for "San Francisco") was founded in 1984 by two then-married Stanford professors—Len Bosack and Sandy Lerner—who could not communicate over the university's clustered network. The routers and software their company came to produce allow computers on different networks (and running different operating systems) to communicate.

Cisco was to the 1990s what Microsoft was to the 1980s and IBM to the 1970s: a company with the right technology at the right time.

clean

Adjective used to describe bug-free code and elegant, transparent design.

CLEC

Pronounced "sea-leck," and short for **competitive local-exchange carrier**. After years of market dominance, the **ILECs—incumbent local-exchange carriers** like regional telcos SBC and Bell Atlantic—are under pressure from upstarts entering the market with advanced data and broadband services. Call them CLECs and blame them for ripping up the streets of every business district to lay fiber, wire large office buildings, and then aggressively sell their slightly cheaper service.

click

This reflex of digital life has clicked its way into the language: **point and click** is what you do on an icon; a **point-and-click interface** lets you mouse your way through anything; the **click-and-buy concept**, **one-click shopping**, and **cost-per-click** are buzzwords of e-commerce.

The noun **double click** is two words. The verb is hyphenated: **double-click. DoubleClick**, a registered trademark, is but one of the Web ad firms trying to turn clicks into cash.

clickthrough

Not "click-thru." The act of a potential customer clicking on a Web banner ad to reach the marketer's site. When using it as a verb, detach "click" from its preposition: *Coveting the notebook computer, she clicked through the Vaio banner ad to Sony's site.*

The **clickthrough rate**—the measure of pageviews that result in ad clicks—is the online adman's gold standard.

client/server

An adjective describing the network architecture in which a powerful, central computer (server) accepts requests for resources and services from many individual PCs (clients). Clients can share files and access data stored on the server. *Client* refers not to the person at the keyboard but to the machine itself, or to the software that interacts with the server.

Clipper Chip

A national data-encryption standard based on the Skipjack algorithm, developed by the National Security Agency and proposed by the Clinton administration in 1993. By scrambling communications, it would make them unintelligible to all but their intended recipients—and the government. Under this hardware-based, **key escrow** encryption scheme, two federal agencies hold the 80-bit decoder "key" in escrow but use it given the appropriate "legal authority." When the high tech industry and civil liberties groups cried war on Clipper in 1994, and after an engineer devised a method of compromising it, the government abandoned the initiative. But the Clipper mentality survived.

Marc Rotenburg, head of EPIC and a vocal opponent, called the Clipper Chip equal parts "governmental arrogance, technological incompetence, and profound disregard for the rights of citizens," adding, "as an exercise in public policy, it ranks somewhere between the Bay of Pigs and the CIA's experiments with psychics." See **encryption, key escrow.**

closed

The synonym for "proprietary," and a dirty word to hackers and backers of the open source software movement.

-co

Short for "company" and originally used in "telco," the suffix has been co-opted by numerous industries for neologisms like *cableco, dataco, pharmco, searchco,* and *webco.* These read like the kind of cheats that editors use to make headlines fit. Caveat emptorco.

coax

Short for coaxial cable, the standard cable TV wiring. Think of coax (pronounced "co-ax") as the fast lane of the info superdriveway—it's speedier than copper, speedier than DSL, speedier than a T-1.

Cobol

The **Common Business Oriented Language** was designed to perform simple calculations on large data sets. Introduced in 1959, it is still widely used, though much despised by hackers. (The clunky language was written in such a way that nonprogrammers—i.e., managers—would be able to read lines of code to determine whether the programmers had made any mistakes.) The Cobol renaissance, aka the **Y2K bug**, made Cobol programmers hotter than Linux admins.

code

The lines of characters that run our lives.

Programmers write **source code**. Computers read **machine code**. And **binary code** is the DNA of digital life. Programmers are sometimes called **codemasters** or **code warriors**. Also a verb: *Are you coding tonight?*

codec

A **compressor/decompressor** algorithm does just that: it squeezes audio or video data into a file small enough to be sent over the Net and viewed on an average desktop (or smaller) machine. Some codecs are designed to handle audio files, others still images; some are optimized for the Web, others for CD-ROMs.

In the jargon of the wireless industry, codec stands for **coder/decoder** and translates the spoken voice into digital bits.

Comdex

Started in 1978, this hardware and software extravaganza occurs twice a year: in Atlanta or Chicago during the spring and Las Vegas in the fall. It's a one-of-a-kind exercise in wretched excess—a place to be, and be seen. Lurking amid what one writer described as "a jarring urbanscape—Microsoft's cathedral and Vivid Video's porn shop, 3M's Century City tower and Micrographix's armadillo racertrack," you'll find VCs and investors, high tech distributors and peddlers.

compression

A method to store text, data, sound, or images in fewer bits. Rather than store every pixel of a blue square, the computer might store one blue pixel and the dimensions of the square. Compression is carried out by any one of many compression standards: AU, GIF, JBIG, JPEG, MPEG, MP3, PICT, SIT, TIFF, ZIP.

Nicholas Negroponte compares digital compression to the ability to "make freeze-dried cappuccino that is so good that by adding water, it comes back to us as rich and aromatic as any freshly brewed in an Italian café."

CompuServe

Founded in 1969 by H&R Block Inc., CompuServe was once one of the largest online service providers, dominating business and international communities. Membership declined, and in 1998 the tax elves sold the service to America Online.

It's sometimes styled CIS for CompuServe Interactive Service, but we prefer CompuServe; the acronym designates **computer information sciences** in academic circles.

comsat

Industry slang for **communications satellite**. Also called a "bird." The initial-capped Comsat is the nickname of the Communications Satellite Corporation.

LEO satellites—orbiting 500 to 1,000 miles above Earth—are used for communications and spying, while **MEOs**—roaming between 1,000 and 22,300 miles out—give GPS systems their sense of direction. The rest of the heavens belongs to **GEOs**, which beam down television signals, weather reports, and other intelligence. See **LEO**.

Connection Machine

A massively parallel computer designed by Danny Hillis in 1981, and the first milestone in his quest to build a computer "that will be proud of me." Hillis's Thinking Machines Corp. began shipping the supercomputer in 1986, but like massive parallelism in general, the Connection Machine turned out to be a bust.

connectivity

The idea of a "fusion of computing and communications" was first posited by Nobel laureate Arno Penzias, but the word has been drained of all pungency by '90s hypesters.

content provider

Marketing metaterm for companies that "create." Not Web-specific, but the new medium breathed new life into the term. If you want to sound like a writer rather than a Buzzword Bingo player, name the creator: CNET, Wired Digital, Disney.

John Dvorak on content: "I hate the notion of content, because it generalizes the value of creative effort by applying a generic word to it. If you're a writer, you write; if you're a movie producer, you produce movies. Being a content guy doesn't say anything about you. Content is talked about as though it's something you can pick up off the floor and throw together."

convergence

The notion of convergence suggests a world in which those all-powerful forces, the TV and the PC, are merged into a seamless information system. Everything—from *The Simpsons* to stock prices—translates into the universal language of 1s and 0s.

cookie

A unique identifier sent to your computer by a Web server and stored on your hard disk. Comparable to a dry-cleaning ticket or a valet parking stub, this authenticated tag lets a server identify you. Cookie and **magic cookie** are old Unix hacker terms given new life by the Web, or rather, by Lou Montulli, the former Netscape programmer and father of the Web cookie. Marketers seized on cookies as a way of tracking Web visitors.

As a verb, the term refers to tagging users' browsers in order to monitor their browsing: *Levi Strauss cookied participants in its blinking-eye campaign.*

coopetition

Cooperation between competitors is especially common in the computer industry, where companies compete on actual products even as they cooperate on technical standards. Needless to say, coopetition makes antitrust authorities nervous. They have a word for competitors who agree not to compete: cartel.

COPA

Children's Online Protection Act of 1998. See **CDA.**

CORE

One of the players in the domain name melee, the **Council of Registrars** represents the companies in the business of registering domain names. These registrars played second fiddle to the government-appointed Network Solutions until May 1999, when CORE and four other companies were chosen to launch a competitive domain name registry. See **DNS, ICANN, Network Solutions.**

core dump

Major download, brain to brain: *I'll give you a full core dump on the project before I leave for Maui.* Unfiltered, a core dump includes random bits of knowledge in addition to key information. Also: **brain dump.**

Technically, a core dump is a copy of the contents in the **core memory**—so-called because of doughnut-shaped magnets known as "cores."

CP/M

Created in 1973 by Gary Kildall for 8080- and Z80-based microcomputers, **Control Program for Microcomputers** was the first widely popular operating system to control the storage and retrieval of information on floppy disks. In 1974, Kildall and his wife founded Intergalactic Digital Research, and earnings eventually topped $5 million. But CP/M was the original victim of Bill Gates's copycatting—MS-DOS, called by Kildall a "complete rip-off," soon drove CP/M out of the market.

CPM

A carryover from traditional media, **cost per thousand** is a standard measurement of advertising rates. Cost per thousand what? Potential customers. Confused by the M? Think Roman numerals. Think millennium.

C-prompt

In the days of DOS, the immutable **C:** was your computer's invitation to dive into your hard drive.

CPU

Technically, the **central processing unit** is the chip that controls and performs calculations. Often used to refer to the memory as well.

cracker

A criminal or malicious hacker, an intruder who breaks into computer systems, "cracking" them. Crackers might disable a system, delete files, or steal data.

MIT professor Richard Stallman coined the term in the 1970s to distinguish malicious network rogues from true hackers.

crypto

Short for "cryptography," which generally refers to the study of secret codes, puzzles, and ciphers. More specifically, it's the study and use of digital algorithms to encode information. Crypto is the impassioned mission of cypherpunks and the guarded domain of the **NSA**. See **public key cryptography, key escrow**.

From cryptography, meaning coded and secret, we get the combining form and nouns like *cryptogram*, *cryptorebel*, and *cryptosystem*.

CSP

The one-stop-shopping solution for small- and medium-size companies wanting to move online. A **commerce service provider** like PSINet, Concentric, and EarthLink will register domain names and host or design Web sites, in addition to providing basic Net service. Spell out CSP on first reference.

CTO

As corporate strategy and corporate networks have become increasingly intertwined, the acronym for **chief technical officer** has become as recognizable as CEO.

While there's no industry standard for titles, **CIO** (chief information officer) is another suit-who-runs-the-systems.

currencies

Express monetary amounts in the currency of the relevant country involved. It doesn't make much sense, for example, to say the

French government spent $76 million to develop a national cable infrastructure. The French spend francs (or euros). Say they spent *f* 395 million and then convert that amount into the currency of your primary audience (in *Wired*'s case, US dollars): *the French government spent 395 million francs (US$76 million*).

Since the dollar is the currency in several countries, always precede the dollar sign with the correct country abbreviation: US$1 million, Ch$75, NZ$250.

cyber-

The terminally overused prefix for all things online and digital. Over the millennia, the word evolved from the Greek *kybernan* (to steer, govern) to Norbert Wiener's *cybernetics* (the science of control and communication) to William Gibson's *cyberspace* (the hallucinatory world existing between computers).

Close up cyberwords: *cybersex, cyberwonk, cyberpunk*. But let cyber stand alone for a compound like *cyber rights*, with its echoes of *civil rights* and *equal rights*.

cyber rights

Civil rights on the Net. Where democracy overlaps with technology. Think encryption, digital privacy, Net censorship.

The many cyber rights organizations include: the **Center for Democracy and Technology** (CDT is a Capitol Hill watchdog founded by Jerry Berman in 1994); **Computer Professionals for Social Responsibility** (the influence of CPSR, the first cyber rights org, faded after the DC arm split off in 1994 to become EPIC); the **Electronic Frontier Foundation** (founded by Mitch Kapor and John Perry Barlow in 1990, the EFF is no longer *the* cyber rights organization); and the **Electronic Privacy Information Center** (the militant wing of cyber rights, led by Marc Rotenburg, David Sobel, and David Banisar and better known as EPIC).

cybernetics

The study of control mechanisms in both man and machine. Derived from the Greek *kybernetes*, meaning governor, the term was seized by Norbert Wiener as the title for his 1948 book. ("Use the word 'cybernetics,' Norbert, because nobody knows what it means. This will always put you at an advantage in arguments," Claude Shannon, the father of information theory, urged the author.)

Wiener's followers saw cybernetics as a science that would explain the world as a set of feedback systems, allowing rational control of bodies, machines, factories, communities, whatever. Wiener's dream—a universal science of communication and control—has faded, though it helped shape such fields as cognitive science.

cyberpunk

Postmodern pulp. Science fiction genre in which high tech goes lowlife and technology invades mind and body and redefines time and space. As Katie Hafner and John Markoff explain in *Cyberpunk:* "High-tech rebels live in a dystopian future, a world dominated by technology and beset by urban decay and overpopulation. It's a world defined by infinitely powerful computers and vast computer networks that create alternative universes filled with electronic demons. Interlopers travel through these computer-generated landscapes . . . [making] their living buying, selling, and stealing information."

Also called The Movement, Radical Hard SF, the Mirrorshade Group, the Eighties Wave, the Outlaw Technologists, or the Neuromantics, the cyberpunk canon includes William Gibson's *Neuromancer*, Neal Stephenson's *Snow Crash*, and Rudy Rucker's *Software*, as well as just about anything written by Bruce Sterling or John Shirley. Then there are the movies—*Blade Runner*, *The Terminator*, and *The Matrix*.

cyberspace

Information space. The ether. The place between phones, between computers, between you and me.

William Gibson in his 1984 science fiction novel *Neuromancer* described cyberspace as the "consensual hallucination experienced daily by billions of legitimate operators, in every nation, by children being taught mathematical concepts. . . . A graphic representation of data abstracted from the banks of every computer in the human system. Unthinkable complexity. Lines of light ranged in the nonspace of the mind, clusters and constellations of data. Like city lights, receding."

In the following years, the term grew beyond its SF roots to become a synonym for the Net—Usenet veteran Keith Lynch dates the first use of cyberspace in this sense to March 1991.

cybersquatter

The speculators of cyberspace, cybersquatters buy up Internet domain names derived from popular words, products, or celebrity names in the hope of reselling them later. Unless, of course, they're journalists like Josh Quittner, who bought mcdonalds.com to give Ronald an ulcer.

cyberstation

A short-lived term—coined circa 1994—for a Web site that is less like a collection of static homepages and more like a live broadcasting network with its own community.

cyborg

Short for **cybernetic organism**. Half machine, half human, like the Six Million Dollar Man and the Bionic Woman. Dr. Manfred Clynes and Nathan Kline coined the term in a 1960 paper, "Cyborgs and Space," though the idea goes back to Mary Shelley's Frankenstein.

Donna Haraway defined cyborgs in "A Cyborg Manifesto": "By the late 20th century, our time, a mythic time, we are all chimeras, theorized and fabricated hybrids of machine and organism."

cypherpunk

Crypto with an attitude. A radical geek or online denizen who is pro-privacy and pro-cryptography (and often supports libertarianism and anarcho-capitalism). The term is derived from the Cypherpunks, an informal group founded by Tim May, Eric Hughes, and John Gilmore in late 1992 and centered around an electronic mailing list.

daemon

A program that runs continuously and automatically in the background. A daemon might handle email received by a network server or respond to requests from other computers on the network. The term derives from the classical Greek word for "a supernatural being," though it was later explained as a shortening of "Disk And Execution MONitor."

Although *daemon* and *demon* are often used interchangeably, the ever-precise Jargon File makes a slight distinction: "demons are usually processes within a program, while daemons are usually programs running on an operating system."

Darpa

Spurred by Sputnik, the Department of Defense established the **Advanced Research Projects Agency** (**Arpa**) in 1958 with a mission to fund high tech R&D. The original name changed in 1972 to **Defense Advanced Research Projects Agency**, pronounced "dar-pah." The "Defense" was deleted in 1993 to reflect the administration's interest in dual-use technologies but was reinstated in 1996.

The organization's greatest legacy may be the **Arpanet**, the experimental packet-switching network—built with US$1 million in 1972—that is the mother of all networking.

Neither Darpa nor Arpa takes an article.

DAT

Pronounced "dat," **digital audiotape** is a high-quality audio recording and storage medium developed by Sony in the mid-'80s.

data

Once there was a day when *datum* was singular and *data* was plural. That day is past. *Datum* is beyond vestigial. "Data is what we do at Dataquest," says Randy Frey, director of editing for that company. Like Frey, treat **data** as a collective noun (it's often used as a synonym for "information") and combine it with a singular verb. And remember: data travels *over* wires or lines, not *through* them.

data mining

Extracting knowledge from information. By teasing useful data out of everything from supermarket buying patterns to credit histories, clever marketeers can compile simple mailing lists or sophisticated psychographic profiles of potential customers. Avoid the solid spelling: "datamine" just looks too pharmaceutical.

DBS

Heavenly television. A high-bandwidth digital TV option, **direct broadcast satellite** is still the underdog to cable, though providers DirecTV and EchoStar are fighting hard. On first reference, spell out the term for this beam-it-up service.

Note: the similar acronym **DSS**, for **direct** or **digital satellite system**, it refers to the equipment needed to receive DirecTV broadcasts.

Deep Blue

Garry Kasparov's silicon adversary in the battle for chess supremacy. IBM's massively parallel computer, built in 1992, can evaluate 200 million chess moves per second and is significantly more powerful than its Carnegie Mellon predecessor, Deep Thought. Deep Blue bested Kasparov in a May 1997 tournament. (FWIW, Claude Shannon built the first chess-playing computer at MIT in 1949.)

demo

A short demonstration of a product or prototype. The proper noun Demo refers to the annual conference run by Stewart Alsop and David Coursey, in association with *InfoWorld*. (It rivals Esther Dyson's PC Forum.) As a verb, to show a demo. Past tense: **demo'd.** Gerund: **demoing.**

DES

Developed at IBM and adopted as a federal standard in 1976, the 56-bit key **data encryption standard** was cracked by crypto activists at the EFF in 1998. Because of its weakness, the security-insecure apply the DES cipher three times, so that information is triple-encrypted—a solution known as

triple DES. The federal standards body has promised to deliver a stronger algorithm by 2002. (See **AES.**)

Like **PGP**, **RSA**, and other encryption schemes, DES is considered a munition by the Feds and is illegal to export. The acronym, too, is a little risky: you might want to identify this standard as the DES crypto system, since DES can also refer to an infamous drug (diethylstilbestrol).

desktop

As a noun, the physical space on a desk, or the virtual space on your computer screen where icons representing hard drives, files, and applications reside. As an adjective—as in *desktop computer*—it suggests an approximate size: bigger than a laptop, smaller than a piece of furniture.

The term **desktop publishing** was coined by Paul Brainerd, who developed PageMaker.

dial up

The verb (plus particle) refers to the traditional way to log on to a network by establishing a phone connection between your computer and your service provider. Keep it two words—"dialupping" would be a disaster. But close up the adjective: a **dialup** account is used by a host computer to verify that the user should be let into the system.

Difference Engine

Designed by Charles Babbage in the 1820s (and partially constructed in 1832), the Difference Engine was the first successful automatic calculator. This icon from the prehistory of computers was inspired by the Jacquard loom. The Difference Engine in turn inspired the 1991 book of the same name, in which authors Bruce Sterling and William Gibson muse over how steam-powered computers would have given us a different history.

The **Analytical Engine**, designed by Babbage and Ada Lovelace in 1837, was conceived as a general-purpose mechanical computer.

digerati

Coined by *New York Times* editor Tim Race, this is the term for the digital elite—the powerful engineers, Third Wave intellectuals, and power brokers of the wired world. Always plural. First appeared in a January 1992 article that Race edited by *Times* reporter John Markoff.

William Safire seized upon the neologism in his Sunday column: "Literati, Italian for the Latin *litterati*, means 'the intellectual set.' In the late 1930s, a portmanteau word was formed to blend the world of glittering celebrities with these intellectuals: glitterati. Now all that glitters is digital, from the Latin for 'finger,' and later applied to a number that can be counted on the 10 fingers. Hence, digerati, 'computer intellectuals,' a word sure to flash through the world's electronic mailboxes."

digital

Strictly speaking, digital refers to the way information is stored as a string of 1s and 0s or any other pair of symbols that represent "on" and "off." This is in contrast to analog, which represents data in a stream of continuous physical variables.

For a quick and simplistic visual explanation, think of digital as black and white, and analog as shades of gray. Digital info can be stored, retrieved, and copied more easily, though it can lack the subtleties of analog.

The word *digital*, meaning in a wired state, exploded in the '90s as a modifier and metaphor. George Orwell would consider it "worn-out."

Digital

Call it what you will—Digital, Digital Equipment Corporation, or DEC (pronounced "deck")—this is the company founded in 1957 by Ken Olsen, one of the engineers of the Whirlwind. Digital's creation of the minicomputer in the 1970s helped set the stage for the PC revolution. In February 1998, Compaq announced a deal to buy Digital for US$9.6 billion, making the merged giant the Number Two computer maker (behind IBM).

digital age

Is it an age? Is it hype? When did it start? We asked around:

Steve G. Steinberg: "I'd say the digital age started in 1972, with the invention of *Pong*. But I'm sure few would agree with me. Other possible points: when binary was first written about by Leibniz in the 1600s (OK, maybe not), when Claude Shannon wrote his paper on information theory in the 1940s, or when the ENIAC was developed in 1946."

Jon Katz: "I've always thought Orson Welles and Walter Winchell unveiled the digital age, setting in motion the philosophy and technology that ultimately led to interactive, outspoken, and innovative fusions of media, technology, and culture. Winchell with his staccato radio broadcasts, Welles with his provocative use of radio, film, and theater as a means of engaging and provoking his audiences."

Vint Cerf: "One cannot really pinpoint a start for the digital age, only a series of events marking its evolution and impact. The transistor was invented sometime around 1947 and the first integrated circuit in 1958—seminal moments. One is tempted to suggest the invention of the single-chip computer as a defining event, but I suspect one has to stick with the transistor as the critical step. Another important date: 1984 and the Apple personal computer, though this was preceded by the MITS Altair, the Xerox PARC Alto, and others."

Pamela McCorduck: "The dawn of the digital age? It was just the way my friends and I lived (we had an old clattering teletype up in the spare room back in 1971, along with an acoustic coupler!). It felt sweet and private and exclusive then: you could actually memorize all the email addresses of anyone you were likely to be in touch with. Time-sharing the mainframe was a very big deal, and clearly the wave of the future instead of batch processing. Back then people got PhDs for doing a text-editing program."

Digital Revolution

It came. It conquered. It got initial capped.

Think of this revolution as the radical reshaping and restructuring of social patterns caused by digital technology. As

Louis Rossetto proclaimed in January 1993: "The Digital Revolution is whipping through our lives like a Bengali typhoon."

By 1998, however, the typhoon had ended: "Face it—the Digital Revolution is over," wrote Nicholas Negroponte. "Extrapolating bandwidth, processor speed, network dimensions, or the shrinking size of electromechanical devices has become truly tiresome. Moore's Law . . . is indeed a stroke of brilliance, but one more mention of it should make you puke. Terabit access, petahertz processors, planetary networks, and disk drives on the heads of pins will be . . . they'll just be."

Dilbert

What Dagwood was to the '60s, Dilbert is to the '90s. The comic strip created by Scott Adams in 1989 produced a mascot for the world of cubicle workers.

Also a verb: **to be Dilberted** is to be exploited by your boss.

dir

DOS-speak for **directory**.

disc and **disk**

Thanks to the different worldviews of the music and computer industries, we are stuck with two words that defy logical distinction. Here are our general guidelines:

disc—an optical-storage medium that is generally round and made of nonmagnetic metal, coated in plastic, and covered with small pits designed to be read from and written to by laser. These silvery platters are used for the CD (compact disc), CD-ROM (the compact disc–read-only memory), the laserdisc, and the digital versatile disc.
disk—a small, flat, portable piece of plastic embedded with magnetic material (a floppy disk) or a less-portable metal-encased storage disk (a hard disk) coated with a magnetic material. A disk is rewritable—you can add digital data to it.
diskette—interchangeable term for floppy.
floppy disk—introduced by IBM in 1971 (it measured 8 inches and was indeed floppy), the floppy disk has become increasingly rigid. It has also become increasingly small, shrinking in

size to 5.25 inches, then to 3.5 inches, and smaller. Also just **floppy**. The plural is **floppies.**

hard disk—the entire storage mechanism (usually located inside a computer) that includes magnetic disks used to store data. Often used interchangeably with **hard drive**, though the two are technically different—the hard disk is located in the hard drive.

Today there are magneto-optical discs/disks that don't fit cleanly into either category.

disintermediation

The Internet works its magic and—poof!—go all the middlemen. Or so the disintermediataries say. In reality, the Net is a maze of intermediaries and the term is a mouthful of jargon.

distributed system

Cooperation by another name. A method by which processing, storage, and other computing tasks are divided among machines. Collections of medium-powered computers sharing work often outperform even high-powered monolithic mainframes.

The network philosophy—and its ultimate realization in the Internet, which with 91 million computers is by far the largest distributed system ever built—powered other phenomena. In "distributed journalism" (also "distributed media") everyone is both a reporter and a consumer of news, and truth is arrived at by acclamation, consensus, conventional wisdom, and gossip. "Distributed intelligence" is management-speak for an organization in which decision-making is decentralized.

DNS

The **domain name system** is the international network of Internet domain servers, names, and addresses. It is currently in a state of flux. For years, .com, .org, .net, and .edu domain names were assigned by Network Solutions, whose current contract with the US government expires in 2000. The Internet Corporation for Assigned Names and Numbers, a nonprofit international private corporation, is building the new global, competitive DNS, involving multiple **Internet registries** (IRs). See **CORE**, **domain name**, **ICANN**, **InterNIC**, **Network Solutions**.

doc

Or **docs**—even in reference to one. Short for **documentation**, the *Gray's Anatomy* of a software program is intended to help users, testers, and later programmers understand how a piece of code works. It seldom does.

A ".doc" at the end of a file name signifies a Microsoft Word document.

domain name

A network name associated with an organization, such as whitehouse.gov or you_pick_the_word.com. Domain names are organized in a hierarchical system, with each level separated by a dot. In the US, the hierarchies are defined by type of entity: commercial (.com), educational (.edu), organizational (.org), governmental (.gov), military (.mil), or network (.net), with new designations like .rec, .shop, and .web being contemplated.

One domain might include hundreds of machines, each with an individual IP address, the numeric identifier—such as 206.221.206.188—of a specific machine on a network.

In the US, most Internet addresses follow a set format: name_of_server.name_of_organization.type_of_organization. The domain name for the headquarters of the Air Combat Command at Langley Air Force Base in Virginia, for example, is acc.af.mil.

Outside the US, most Net addresses appear as server_name.organization_name.country_code, with the **top-level domain** being a country code. The American University in Cairo's academic computing services domain, for example, is auc-acs.eun.eg (.eun stands for Egyptian Universities Network). These country codes are defined in an international standards document and distributed by the Internet Society. (You can find the most up-to-date list at *www.isoc.org/internet/infrastructure/connectivity/country.shtml.*)

See **DNS**.

Doom

The kill-or-be-killed 3-D computer game that became a modern classic. When id Software released a shareware version of the game over the Net in 1993, a generation of gamers was hooked. The *Doom* genre includes *Quake* and *Duke Nukem*.

DOS

Although DOS—pronounced "doss"—is used in the name of several competing systems that incorporate storage disks, the acronym for **disk operating system** is most often used in reference to MS-DOS, the software (originally PC-DOS) that launched the Microsoft empire and became the most widely installed PC operating system in the world. Until Windows, that is.

Don't say "DOS system"!

.

The period symbol is used in email addresses, URLs, and newsgroups to separate constituent parts. But in this context, it's called a **dot.**

.com

The Inc., Ltd., and Bros. of Internet business. Note the stream of .com companies: Drugstore.com, Buy.com, Beyond.com, even Pets.com. Entrepreneurs and writers alike have seized on this top-level domain as the hip suffix of digital existence. Note Sun Microsystems' ad campaign "We're the dot in .com," and Po Bronson's reference to the "obfuscating dot-com jargon of the Valley." Financial types, in their enthusiasm for the **dotcom** segment of the market, spell out the "dot" and close up the compound.

download

To copy a document or application from a network or server to a personal computer. Usage has spread to the colloquial, where *to download* may simply mean *to absorb*.

And download this: in a 1997 *New Yorker* article, Ken Auletta wrote that Netscape "downloaded its browser on the Web." Wrong. The company *uploaded* its software *to* the Web, where we all could download it to our computers.

dpi

A measurement of image resolution, **dots per inch** is lowercase and never spelled out.

drag and drop

Drop the hyphens for the noun, but retain them for the drag-and-drop world of adjectives.

Drudge, Matt

The controversial figurehead of online journalism—less reporter than gossiper—made a name for himself through the Monica Lewinksy scandal. But Drudge is hardly Woodward *or* Bernstein. White House aide Sidney Blumenthal filed a US$30 million libel suit against him in 1997, and the vituperative writer Michael Wolff defined Drudge journalism as "the publication or dissemination of facts that no other media will publish." *New York Times* writer Francis X. Clines was more charitable, calling Drudge simply a "Walter Winchell wannabe."

Drudgery is a coinage for "Net muckraking."

DSL

This modem and compression technology squeezes multiple channels of multimedia data—fast—down standard copper phone lines. DSL stands for **digital subscriber line** or **loop**. (Hint: *loop* is correct for the protocol; *line* for the wires.) The primary competition to cable modems, DSL boasts connections up to 50 times faster than a dialup modem and eight times faster than ISDN, though the actual speeds depend on how close you are to the telephone switching-center.

The acronym sometimes appears as **xDSL**, in reference to the myriad versions of the technology. **ADSL** transmits data downstream faster than it travels upstream (the "A" is for **asymmetric**). **SDSL** provides a **symmetrical DSL** connection, sending and receiving data at the same speeds.

DSP

A filter for wireless communications, a **digital signal processing** circuit separates the signal from the noise. Think of removing the echo on a song's vocal track, or color correction on a video signal. Several different DSP techniques exist.

DTV

A grab-all term for the error-free, easy-to-compress, highly flexible, sharper TV pictures and sound achieved by sending signals in digital bits rather than in analog radio waves. The various guises of **digital television** include **DBS**, **digital HDTV**, **SDTV** (standard definition TV).

DVD

Née **digital video disk**, DVD launched in '97 as a new-and-improved way to see home movies. In a manufacturer's makeover, the "video" became "versatile," the "disk" became "disc," and DVD was reintroduced as a high-density CD format—used to store music, films, or software. In this sense, **digital versatile disc** is sometimes referred to as **DVD-ROM** and played in the DVD-ROM drive of a PC.

dynamically generated pages

These Web creations—birthed at the time they are downloaded, rather than served over and over—often contain up-to-the-second data pulled into a template. A dynamically generated page may respond to a user's location or browser, or it may respond to information provided in a survey form. Search-engine results pages and My Yahoo! pages are both dynamically generated.

Note: dynamically generated Web pages are unrelated to dynamic HTML (see **HTML**).

e-

Short for "electronic," this prefix—er, letter—was named 1998 Word of the Year by the American Dialect Society, as well as Most Useful (ugh!) and Most Likely to Succeed (pity us all). It does seem to be popping up everywhere, from the time-honored **email** to the trademarked **E*Trade** and **eSchwab**, to the too-cutesy **e-tailing**. Save a keystroke and drop the hyphen for email, an unmistakable cultural shift, but for those coinages destined to fade into the ether (eprints) or create unseemly combinations (eart?), keep the hyphen and the vestige of the word *electronic*.

Please, resist the urge to use this vowel-as-cliché. The "eSourcing defined" print ad campaign, which defined "e.maz.ing" as "of or pertaining to . . . a strategic partnership with Eliance," is an example of e-xcessive usage. In "The Hyphenator's Handbook—or—the Hyphen-Hater's Handbook," Peter Neumann points to the linguistic confusion ushered in by too-facile coinages like:

e-lapse [an omission in an electronic communication)
e-merge [to combine different input streams)
e-quality [a property of a computer system or network)
e-quip [humor embedded in e-mail)

eBay

A virtual auction house, eBay turned the ease of click-and-buy into the thrill of click-and-bid. As the number of eBay members (addicts?) exploded, so did the company's stock price, giving the company the valuation it needed to acquire the tony **brick-and-mortar** auction house Butterfield & Butterfield in 1999.

ease of use

Popularized with the advent of the Macintosh, this squishy term should be avoided. Find the synonym that fits the context, like *elegance, simplicity*, or *utility*.

Easter egg

A small cartoon, animation, or other feature hidden by a programmer in the code of a game or application and triggered by an arcane sequence of keystrokes or mouseclicks. Easter eggs are the programmer's equivalent of graffiti tags, a digital version of "Kilroy was here."

Echo

Stacey Horn founded this online salon in 1990. Discussions favor culture, politics, and the life of the mind. Horn has called the more than 3,000 members of the **East Coast Hang Out** "the crankiest group in cyberspace."

e-commerce

Business on the Net. Faster, better, and cheaper. A universal marketplace where everyone, everywhere can pick through the same stall at the same time.

In the short, high-risk history of online business, the most successful ventures have turned established paradigms upside down. More than new business models, the early e-commerce powers are metaphors for a new order in which vision begets a staggering market cap: Amazon.com is a symbol for the power of dematerializing the retail sales point; eBay, an emblem for a world turned into a community of merchandisers; Priceline, a metaphor for restructuring the differential between price and value.

If Amazon's founder Jeff Bezos is the poster boy of e-commerce, Rick Boucher was its founding father: in 1992 this congressional representative from Virginia sponsored an amendment to the National Science Foundation Act of 1950 allowing noneducational—i.e., commercial—activity on the Net.

ego surfing

A term coined by Sean Carton, an interactive media specialist from Baltimore, and Jargon Watch's Gareth Branwyn. The two realized they needed a term for a favorite activity: using search engines to find references to themselves online. Also **egofiltering**.

egoboo

Defined by open source advocate Eric S. Raymond as "pride in seeing one's work appreciated," egoboo is what motivates hackers—and separates the code warriors from the workaday programmers.

electric, electrical, and electronic

Webster's may list the words as synonyms, but not the *IEEE Standard Dictionary of Electrical and Electronics Terms,* which defines **electric** as "containing, producing, arising from, actuated by, or carrying electricity." In contrast, **electrical** means "related to, pertaining to, or associated with electricity but not having its properties or characteristics." Your kitchen stove may be electric, but it was designed by an electrical engineer.

Electronic suggests devices, circuits, or systems using electron devices. As an adjective, **electronics** means "of, or pertaining to, the field of electronics," as in *electronics engineer*. As a plural noun, it refers to "that field of science and engineering that deals with electron devices" and "that branch of science and technology which relates to devices in which conductance is principally by electrons moving through a vacuum, gas, or semiconductor."

Eliza

An early experiment in **artificial intelligence**, Eliza was a computer program that simulated a psychologist. It was created by MIT professor Joseph Weizenbaum and introduced in his 1966 article "ELIZA: A Computer Program for the Study of Natural Language Communication Between Man and Machine."

The descendants of Eliza, those software programs that simulate human speakers, are known today as **chatterbots**. Still in the experimental phase, these conversational bots might soon provide customer service and other information online.

email

A telegraph, a memo, and a palaver rolled into one. Or, as Jon Katz says, "the best form of communication—ever." In 1999, 83 million Americans and 140 million people worldwide claimed email access. More trivia: 100 million email messages are sent every day.

The earliest form of email involved exchanging files in a time-sharing system. The first email as we think of it—a message transmitted over a network—was sent by Ray Tomlinson in 1972. And what was the message? "Oh, if I'd known it was going to be *the* message I would have typed something wittier," Tomlinson says today, "but it probably said 'qwertyuiop' or 'this is a test.' "

Twenty years after the invention of email, the "to hyphen or not to hyphen" debate continues. Some copy editors stick adamantly to the tradition of A-bomb, G-men, and V-chip; others simply argue that the hyphen is necessary to prevent reading the term as em-ail. But increasingly, editors are saying "It's only a matter of time. Get with the program."

When using the word in a compound noun, don't hyphenate the duo either: *email account, email box, email log.*

Email can refer to many email messages, as in *Mr. Boies is using internal email to nail Microsoft.* It can also be a verb: *Email me, or I'll hound you f2f.* Mutations are also popping up: **emailable, emailer.**

embedded system

The chip in the thermostat that adjusts automatically to ambient temperature, the processors in a car that control the transmission and the antilock brakes, the computer in your telephone that operates speed dial—scratch the world's surface and you find computers known as embedded systems.

e-money

Digital cash. The new economy's answer to coins and bills.

Go with the generic noun, though various companies have trademarked E-money, Ecash, CyberCash and other synonyms. Although the word caught on immediately, the adoption of electronic currency has lagged.

emoticons

Treacly expressions of emotion also known as smileys. The noun evolved from the command Emote, used in MUDs to convey actions. See **smileys** for more cheerfulness than you knew existed.

encryption

The source of electronic trust. Tools to keep networks, databases, and files private and secure. Technology that provides a cloak of confidentiality or a mark of identity.

The most common form of encryption uses mathematical algorithms to scramble and unscramble digital messages so that only their intended recipients can read them. Various encryption schemes include standard **private key, public key,** and **key escrow.**

The most widely used public key encryption scheme in the US is **RSA**—introduced in 1978, named after its inventors Ronald Rivest, Adi Shamir, and Leonard Adleman, and owned by RSA Data (now a subsidiary of Security Dynamics Technologies, Inc.). On the Web, the most common security scheme is the SSL (secure sockets layer) protocol designed by Netscape.

Some governments—notably that of the United States—restrict all but the weakest forms of encryption, under the pretext that criminals and terrorists will use it to hide their evil doings.

See also **Clipper Chip, PGP, public key cryptography.**

enhanced

Industry marketing-speak for new-and-improved. Because its "meaning" depends on the context, the adjective does little to enhance your writing.

ENIAC

Built by John W. Mauchly and J. Presper Eckert at the Moore School of Electrical Engineering from 1942 to 1946, the **Electronic Numerical Integrator and Computer** is generally accepted as the first digital electronic computer. Some give the honor to the ABC, or Atanasoff-Berry Computer, a prototype of an electromechanical digital computer built in 1941 by John Atanasoff and Clifford Berry. Still others claim that the Z3, built by German computer scientist Konrad Zuse in 1941, deserves the honor. But the ENIAC, a 30-ton, 18,000-vacuum tube behemoth, remains the sentimental favorite.

Pronounce it "ee-knee-ack," but don't say "ENIAC computer"—that's redundant.

error message

The message from a computer network or program telling you something's amiss and it's up to you to fix it. Some messages are delivered in simple English: *This program has performed an illegal operation and will be shut down.* Others are more cryptic: *An error occurred: —123.*

ether

A metaphor for the online environment, for the Prufrockian world between my email in-box and yours.

Behind the metaphor lie centuries of scientific definitions. Nature abhors a vacuum, proclaimed Aristotle. Something—the ether—must fill the nooks and crannies of the universe, concluded 19th-century scientists. Though Einstein's theory of relativity replaced older theories of ether, some physicists have reclaimed the term, redefining it as "quantum fields." Still, most physicists prefer to call this vacuum "virtual waves."

Ethernet

A high-bandwidth local-area network primarily for personal computers; known by networking geeks as IEEE 802.3 standard. Conceived in a 1973 Xerox PARC memo by Bob Metcalfe and David Boggs and introduced in 1976, Ethernet has achieved ubiquity, though some find it dowdy. Others, like technopundit George Gilder, rave about it: "At its present pace of progress, Ethernet will someday run isochronous (real-time) gigabits per second on linguine."

Trademarked and pronounced "ee-ther-net," it prevailed over token ring to become *the* standard high-speed LAN hardware technology. At the beginning of 1999, there were more than 100 million Ethernets worldwide, allowing uncountable computers to exchange digital data over twisted-pair telephone wires. The Internet is essentially a wide-area network of local-area networks, most of which are 10 Mbps Ethernets.

euro

The new common currency of the European Union. Euro coins and bills enter circulation on January 1, 2002 in 15 nations. Exchange rates can be found at *www.europa.eu.int/euro*. Although the euro has been baptized Europe's common currency, only years of usage will make it the single currency. For now, continental types can't even decide on the plural: the Bank of England counts its *euros*, while Italy's Accademie della Crusca adores its *euri*.

eye candy

Wow factor. The photos and illustrations, animated GIFs and CG creations that make a visual impact. Eye-popping graphics.

eyeballs

Viewers. Audience, especially for a TV show or Web site.

The most-valued currency of an age in which information abounds and attention is scarce.

f2f

Face-to-face. Offline. Refers to communication that is not electronic. Time spent in a living room rather than a chat room is **facetime.** Talking f2f is sometimes called **facemail.**

fab

Chip fabrication becomes **chip fab** becomes **fab.** Unless, of course, a company designs chips but does not produce them, in which case it's a **fabless** semiconductor company.

FANTOM

Email sent by someone other than the owner of the account. These prank messages are typed in caps, hence the uppercase style of the term.

FAQ

A **frequently-asked-questions** file contains everything you ever wanted to know about a Web site, a mailing list, or even a product. It answers the questions asked so often by newbies that veterans and tech support are driven to distraction. FAQs evolved from the Net need for readable, informative, and regularly updated information.

When pronounced "fack," FAQ should be preceded by the indefinite article *a;* when pronouncing each letter, use *an.*

FCC

The **Federal Communications Commission** was created by the Communications Act of 1934 to police the airwaves. Although it's an independent regulatory standards body, the FCC reports directly to Congress. Increasingly, it's become the referee of cyberspace squabbles.

FDDI

Pronounced "fiddy" and standing in for **fiber distributed data interface**, this network architecture offered a faster and more dependable alternative to Ethernet or token ring. These days, though, it has few takers.

fiber optics

A communications technology, invented by Narinder S. Kapany at England's University of Rochester in 1956, that sends electromagnetic signals down cables made of glass or plastic fibers. Hyphenated and singular as an adjective: *fiber-optic cable.* Fiber optics as a mass noun crops up often in telecom talk—it's cheaper than traditional copper wiring, difficult to tamper with, and allows virtually unlimited bandwidth. It transmits in gigabits, while copper deals in megabits.

file extension

A short tag that identifies a file's format and tells what application—which compression software, for instance—is needed to open it.

Extensions appear in lowercase at the end of file names: .aiff, .gif, .html, .hqx, .jpeg, .tar, .z, .zip. In any other reference, style file formats in caps and drop the period: GIF, JPEG, MP3.

file name

Two words, like **screen name** and **domain name**. In the early DOS days, computers wouldn't allow spaces in names and forced users to make file names one word. But *file name* itself was never closed up—in DOS or in English.

file sharing

Allowing multiple users to access data or applications on a network. This contrasts to sharing files by email or **sneakernet** (copying files to a disk and delivering it by foot). File sharing systems—which may limit or specify access—have been around since the mainframe era. See **FTP**.

finger

A command used to gather information about a network user—such as name, logon, office location, phone number, email address, and perhaps account activity. Also a verb. Although originally a Unix term, now many operating systems let you finger a user with a vengeance.

firewall

The wall of software that keeps unauthorized meanderers or malicious intruders outside a network. Sometimes it also keeps employees using an internal company network from browsing the Web.

500-channel universe

The cliché denoting the Promised Land of digital media: the all-you-can-watch Net-TV future.

flame

An inflammatory email or posting, sometimes called "a nastygram," according to the Jargon File. Check out this **.sig file** that came our way: *The Microsoft Network—Finally AOLers have people to flame*. Also commonly used as a verb.

When Ellen Spertus wrote an AI-based flame filter, she developed a set of linguistic rules characterizing flaming: a high incidence of noun phrases as appositions ("you bozos") and the presence of the verb "get," followed within 10 characters by "life," "lost," "real," "clue," "with it," or "used to it."

flavor

An old programming term for *version* or *kind*. These days, the term is most often used in the context of Unix.

flops

Pronounced "flops," **floating-point operations per second** is to a computer what wpm is to a secretary. Don't spell it out. Often combined with a prefix: *kilo-*, *mega-*, *giga-*, *tera-*, *peta-*.

font

Digital calligraphy. A font is defined by typeface (Times Roman, Myriad, Palatino), as well as size, weight, italics, and other characteristics. Here's the fine print: *font* and *typeface* are not synonyms.

Fortran

Created by John Backus at IBM in 1954, and short for **Formula Translator**, the oldest major programming language still in use dominates scientific computing, number crunching, and engineering.

404 Error File Not Found

The Web equivalent of "You have reached a number that has been disconnected or is no longer in service." Used colloquially: "He's 404" means "He's not at his desk and no one knows where he is." Anything 404 is off the grid.

Stylewise, treat this message-box missive as you would treat commands such as Print or Save: capitalize and don't set in quotation marks.

fps

Lowercase, like bps and mph. In fact, think of **frames per second** as the mph of movies and video.

frame

The windowpanes of a Web page. Each frame is built as a separate HTML file and embedded in a master file.

frame relay

A common **WAN** technology, the frame relay is a networking version of interoffice mail. Corporations depend on it to create permanent point-to-point circuit-switched links between office buildings.

Free-Net

Some use the solid *Freenet* for this system of affiliated, open-access community computing networks. We retain the hyphen and caps in honor of the first such network, the Cleveland Free-Net Community Computer System, founded by Tom Grundner in 1984 and closed in 1999. Free-Nets emphasize local information and wide access.

free software

Also called **open source software**, it "comes with permission for anyone to use, copy, and distribute, either verbatim or with modifications, either gratis or for a fee," according to Richard Stallman, the MIT professor and legendary hacker. In 1984, Stallman founded the **Free Software Foundation**, a nonprofit organization that promotes free software as a means to strengthen civil society. He wrote the **GNU** ("GNU's Not Unix") operating system and released it under a copy-and-modify-to-your-heart's-content software license he called "copyleft."

Stallman's mantra: "Think free as in free speech, not free beer."

See **open source, GNU**.

friction-free

What markets want to be. Information technology makes transactions of all kinds smoother by eliminating high transportation costs, poor communications, and parasitic intermediaries—in other words, friction.

frontdoor

The main title or contents page of a Web site. Some tech types once used "front page" as a synonym, but that ended with Microsoft's Front Page, the trademarked product that helps you create and manage a professional-looking Web site even if you don't know what the hell you're doing.

The term can also refer to the standard method of accessing a network.

front end

It's what you see onscreen—the part of the software you interact with. The **back-end** software, on the other hand, runs on a network server or mainframe. Two words as a noun, hyphenated as an adjective.

FTP

A method of transferring files between computers over the Internet. FTP sites are sometimes written in the URL format of the Web—*ftp://artemis.arc.nasa.gov*. Unknown to the majority of Net users, FTP is still the best way to transfer large files. Oh—and **file transfer protocol** is the language computers must speak to do the transaction.

Can also be a verb: you FTP to a site or, if you did it in the past, you **FTP'd**.

FUD

Favorite expression of computer engineers, coined by Gene Amdahl and pronounced "fud." In the software business, instilling **fear, uncertainty, doubt** in consumers—telling them a smaller competitor will not last or its product won't work—gives a company the power to set the agenda.

According to the Jargon File, Gene Amdahl coined the term after he left Big Blue to found his own company: "FUD is the fear, uncertainty, and doubt that IBM salespeople instill in the minds of potential customers who might be considering [our] products."

Fuller, R. Buckminster

Architect, engineer, inventor, and environmentalist, Buckminster Fuller (1895–1983) was the Leonardo da Vinci of the 20th century: his creations include the Dymaxion House, the geodesic dome, and numerous transportation machines. Bucky, as he was called by fans, often introduced himself as "the world's most successful failure," and indeed many of his projects went unrealized, but his life and legacy inspired a generation of inventors.

The C60 molecule Buckminsterfullerene (aka the **buckyball**) was discovered in 1985 and named in homage to Bucky's work in geodesics.

functionality

Use sparingly, if at all. Better to say "its functions" or "its features." Or recraft your sentence: "X does A, B, and C."

Future Shock

Alvin Toffler coined the term in a 1965 article (and wrote the book in 1970) to describe people's reactions and maladjustments to the rapid technological changes that swept society after World War II. Toffler's portentous opener reads: "This is a book about what happens to people when they are overwhelmed by change."

FWIW

An online equivocation, meaning **for what it's worth**.

f/x

Shorthand for **special effects**, and pronounced "eff-ex," this stands for smoke and mirrors on the silver screen. The technologies—motion capture, key-frame animation, and animatronics, among others—that suspend disbelief and empower the dinosaurs in *Jurassic Park*, the plunging *Titanic*, the sleek Gungan warriors of *The Phantom Menace*.

FYFS

A short retort—**fuck you for sharing**—from an online crank.

gameplay

The videogame equivalent of how a car handles, gameplay involves a combination of factors: Are the controls intuitive? Does the program respond to the player's actions? Is it addictive or will it end up on the shelf? A title's graphics and sound might suck, but it can still give good gameplay.

It is spelled solid, along with other terms from the gaming world: **gameplayer** (such as Sony's PlayStation 2, Sega's Dreamcast, and the Nintendo Ultra 64) and **gamebox** (another word for the system hardware)—but not **Game Boy** (Nintendo's ever-successful handheld).

gateway

A translator machine or router that links networks speaking different protocols. Email sent from AOL to the Internet passes through a mail gateway. When you add an initial cap, you get **Gateway Computers**, the South Dakota–based PC manufacturer that ships its econo-PCs in Holstein-inspired boxes.

geek

Someone who codes for fun, speaks Unix among friends, and reads Slashdot daily.

Hardly a digital-age coinage, the term has roots in English dialect and came to mean a carnival or circus performer who committed loathsome acts. Biting the head off of a chicken, say. Be wary of too-freely tossing the term about; it's considered a putdown when uttered by a nongeek.

genomics

This term for the study of genes and their functions springs from **genome**. Genomics promises to give humans veto power over their DNA, along with vexing ethical problems.

The international Human Genome Project, an ambitious initiative launched in October 1990, aims to sequence and map the 60,000 to 80,000 genes of the human genome by early in the 21st century.

GIF

Use the acronym, and pronounce it "giff" ("jif" is for the peanut butter). The **graphic interchange format** is a compression format for images. It can be a verb, as in *Have you GIF'd the Pamela Anderson video stills yet?*

In the context of a file name it appears in the standard lowercase format: fetish.gif.

GNU

Pronounced "guh-new" and standing for **GNU's Not Unix**, this open source Unix-workalike developed by Richard Stallman's **Free Software Foundation** hoped to be a better, freer version of that ubiquitous OS. In reality, GNU provided the spirit of the open source movement, but Linux, built on the shoulders of GNU, became the open source Unix of choice. See **free software, open source.**

gopher

A relic of early Net days, gopher was named after the mascot of the University of Minnesota, where it was developed in April 1991. The protocol provided a seamless interface to transfer files, browse databases, and telnet to sites around the Internet, simply and easily. As with other tools like telnet, gopher is treated as a generic term and styled lowercase.

GPS

The **global positioning system** is a constellation of satellites operated by the US Department of Defense. For the cost of a VCR, you can hold a palm-size GPS device that will calculate your exact latitude, longitude, and altitude.

grayscale

A kind of monitor. Not black and white. Not color. Some companies spell it "greyscale," but since when did Silicon Valley defer to the British on spelling? Don't make the weighty mistake of separating the syllables: a *gray scale* belongs on your bathroom floor, not on your desk.

grep

An abbreviation for "get regular expression," grep is Unix for advanced text search. Colloquially, *to grep* means "to search": *Grep the email for suspicious headers.*

grok

A verb meaning to scan all available information regarding a situation, digest it, and form a distilled opinion.

Grok is an example of language that has percolated from fiction into life. Tom Wolfe grokked *grok* in *The Electric Kool-Aid Acid Test.* Years earlier, Robert A. Heinlein dreamed up the term in that SF favorite, *Stranger in a Strange Land.*

Strictly, grok meant "to drink or taste": "Jubal took the spoon and tasted the broth. . . . [T]he flavor was sweet and could have used salt. 'But let's grok him as he is.'" But even Heinlein used the word metaphorically: "He found both butterflies and women tremendously interesting—in fact, all the grokking world around him was enchanting and he wanted to drink so deep of it all that his own grokking would be perfect."

Like Heinlein, double the consonant in **grokked** and **grokking**.

GSM

The European cell-phone standard, **global system for mobile** (communications) resembles the TDMA standards common in the US. But **3G**, the next-generation GSM—which keeps simultaneous conversations flowing by encoding the bits—hews closer to the up-and-coming CDMA technology. See **CDMA**, **cell phone**, **TDMA**, **wireless**.

GUI

Pronounced "gooey," and standing for **graphical user interface**, this breakthrough was brought to us by Xerox PARC and SRI International, where it was developed in the early 1970s under the name of **Wimp** (for "window, icon, menu, pointing device"). It was popularized by the Mac in the 1980s.

GUIs turned computing into a visual treat, replacing text commands and function keys with icons, windows, and that staging area called the desktop. Of course, hackers, Unix wizards, and some reticent academics still cling to the Alt-F5s and greps of command-line existence.

Gutenberg

The name of Johannes Gutenberg, who invented movable type (*not* the printing press) around 1450 and published the Gutenberg Bible by 1456, conjures the birth of publishing and the rise of literacy and mass media.

Gutenberg's innovation has been seized as a metaphor by digital mavens and media critics, from Marshall McLuhan (author of *The Gutenberg Galaxy*, 1962) to Sven Birkerts (author of *The Gutenberg Elegies: The Fate of Reading in an Electronic Age*, 1994). Then there's the **Gutenberg Project**, begun in 1971 by Michael Hart with the goal of digitizing 10,000 texts by the year 2001. More than 2,000 "e-texts" were online in the spring of 1999.

A **gutenberg**, according to Gareth Branwyn's Jargon Watch, is the office Luddite who insists on printing out documents rather than reading them onscreen.

hack

To work on a project. At MIT, the word can also mean to pull a prank on someone or to explore the dark tunnels and air shafts of an institutional building.

As a noun, it denotes a solution. Steven Levy, in *Hackers*, describes a hack as "a project undertaken or a product built not solely to fulfill some constructive goal, but with some wild pleasure taken in mere involvement . . . a feat imbued with innovation, style, and technical virtuosity." A *good hack* is synonymous with clever, *bad hack* with shoddy.

Although hacking is most often used in the computer context, it can refer to any deft work. As Katie Hafner and John Markoff explain in *Cyberpunk*, "a palindromic music composition was considered a good hack (thus making Haydn, with his Palindrome Symphony, an honorary hacker)."

hacker

Skilled computer programmer or engineer who loves a challenge. Not synonymous with "computer criminal" or "security breaker." (Hackers hate hacks who call crackers hackers.)

Emmanuel Goldstein (aka Eric Corley, editor of that hands-on guide to phone hacking, *2600*) had this to say on the difference between hackers, crackers, and phreakers: "A **hacker** is anyone who asks a lot of questions, refuses to accept simplistic dead-end answers, is willing to bend rules to attain knowledge, and has a real sense of adventure. **Cracker** is a term invented by older hackers in a misguided attempt to separate themselves from behavior they consider 'juvenile.' A **phreaker** is someone who plays with the phone system, which means that they have hacker blood in them."

Hacker Ethic

When hacker culture developed at MIT in the '50s and '60s, a certain philosophy began to emerge. As Steven Levy writes, "the precepts of this revolutionary Hacker Ethic were not so much debated and discussed as silently agreed upon." They included:

- Access to computers—and anything that might teach you something about the way the world works—should be unlimited and total. Always yield to the Hands-On Imperative!
- All information should be free.
- Mistrust Authority—Promote Decentralization.

- Hackers should be judged by their hacking, not bogus criteria such as degrees, age, race, or position.
- You can create art and beauty on a computer.
- Computers can change your life for the better.

HAL

The omnipotent onboard computer that symbolized the fear of a machine-controlled future in Stanley Kubrick and Arthur C. Clarke's seminal 1968 film *2001: A Space Odyssey*.

Rumor holds that HAL's name derived from combining each of the preceding letters of IBM. However, Kubrick and Clarke offered a different explanation in the book version: "The sixth member of the crew . . . was not human. It was the highly advanced HAL 9000 computer, the brain and nervous system of the ship (Heuristically programmed ALgorithmic computer, no less)."

handheld

Smaller than a desktop. As an adjective, it describes a graspable device. As a noun, it refers to portable digital devices. But the technical definition is fuzzy, so get specific by using the brand name rather than the buzzword: 3Com's Palm VII, Philip's Nino, Compaq's Aero.

handle

Online name. Borrowed from the world of CB radios. Treat it like a regular name (i.e., use roman type) and don't muck with the user's case or punctuation: Mr_Bungle. Handles can be as fun to interpret as vanity license plates: FeABS (abs of steel), AuTOUCH (golden touch), or 6ULDV8 (sexual deviate).

handshake

The time spent by two modems or computers murmuring hellos and good-byes. Computers making a connection must establish the protocols, figure out what language they are speaking, and compute how fast each is talking before they can begin the conversation and start transmitting data.

HDTV

After the original analog **high-definition television** technology stalled in the US, government and industry united to develop a digital standard, deliverable via satellite, cable, or old-fashioned broadcast. But the high-resolution technology hasn't taken off: consumers won't spend megabucks for an HDTV set until there's HDTV programming, broadcasters won't develop programming until there's an audience. And even then, broadcasters would rather use the power of digital to deliver lucrative data services. HDTV is all looks and no brains compared to some digital TV technologies. See **DTV**.

high-order bit

The ur-bit.

Technically, it is the bit with the highest value in a binary number (in a decimal analogy, the high-order bit of "1,500,004" would be the "1").

Colloquially, it is the one-minute chunk of a 30-minute conversation that really matters. In the Valley, *I just want the high-order bit* means "Get to the point and don't waste my time." Also synonymous with "takeaway," "big idea," or "priority" as in: *The high-order bit is that we get this deal done. I don't care what the cost is.*

high tech

Yes, we know you know what this phrase means. But we're here to tell you that since *high tech* is as ubiquitous as *high school,* we don't think the adjective needs a hyphen: go with *high tech company, high tech industry*, or *high tech innovation.* But, please, don't go with *hi tech*, *hi-tech*, or *Hi-tech.*

high touch

Coined by John Naisbitt in his book *MegaTrends,* the term describes half of the "high tech/high touch" trend: the more we are surrounded by computers and technology, the more we crave tactile things that provide comfort and services that involve frequent, personal interactions. Naisbitt's 1999 book *High Tech•High Touch* expands on his theories about the co-evolution of technology, culture, art, and spirituality.

hit

Technically, a computer's request for an image or file from a Web server. In the early Web days, hits were a common measure of a site's popularity. But since the text on a page is one hit, and the accompanying JPEG another, hits have been abandoned as a demographic tool. CEOs now talk of **pageviews**.

homepage

The homepage is the most basic building block of the Web and the quaint, mom-and-pop precursor to the Internet economy's online malls. A homepage can announce a baby's birth or post a résumé; it can serve as the frontdoor to an extensive Elvis fan club; it can help hawk anything from exotic teas to erotic T-shirts.

John Seabrook, writing in *The New Yorker*, calls the personal homepage "a new kind of private space within the public space of the network . . . a place on the Net where people can find you . . . a front porch. You can design your page in any way you wish, and furnish it with anything that can be digitized—your ideas, your voice, your causes, pictures of your scars or your pets or your ancestors."

Traditionalists hewing to the rules of compounding (two words, equal stress, don't compress) would style the term open. But we think the two syllables combine to form one idea. Besides, we like the frontier echoes of *homestead*.

host

A computer on a network that provides a service or information to other computers. A machine may be known on the network by its **hostname** or by its IP address.

The term even inspired this engineering student jingle (sung to the tune of the *Mr. Ed* theme song): "A host is a host, from coast to coast. And no one will talk to a host that's close, unless the host that isn't close is busy, hung, or dead."

hotspot

A clickable area onscreen. On a Web page, an image, icon, or button with an embedded link. As two words, "hot spot" misleadingly suggests disco balls, stylish cocktails, and a place to be seen. But a hyperlinked image map on the Web is not a spot that is hot, it is a hotspot, a compound word whose distinct technical meaning requires the solid spelling.

For consistency's sake, *hotlink* should also be closed. But for brevity's sake, we shorten hotlink to **link**. That also avoids confusion with sausage.

HP

An old-line, if a little unglamorous, computer manufacturer, **Hewlett-Packard Company** was founded—in the prototypical garage—by Stanford alums William Hewlett and David Packard in 1938. In 1949, the pair built a breakthrough audio oscillator (a tool for testing sound quality) that was first used by Disney for the production of *Fantasia*. Government orders boosted the company's fortunes during World War II, and HP entered the Fortune 500 way back in 1962.

In a March 1999 makeover, HP (by now a diversified Fortune 50 company) spun its measurement equipment business into a new company—Agilent Technologies—retaining the HP name for its computer and printer divisions.

HP is known in the Valley and elsewhere as the original well-run company, a daunting competitor, a model of philanthropy, and a breeding ground for high tech CEOs. Use the abbreviated name: HP is as recognizable as IBM or Apple.

HTML

The formatting lingo of the Web, **hypertext markup language** lets humans talk to Web servers and browsers. HTML is spoken in **tags**—short commands such as <H1> that surround pertinent text like quotation marks: <H1> write your headline here </H1>.

Also used as a verb: *Have you HTML'd the column yet?*

DHTML, or **dynamic HTML**, incorporates scripting languages and multimedia elements (such as moving menus and changing colors) into a Web page.

HTTP

The original communications protocol of the Web. Browsers use **hypertext transfer protocol** to connect to Web servers, and servers use HTTP to talk amongst themselves. The acronym is OK, but note that it appears in all caps when used as a noun in text, lowercase as part of a URL—*http://www.cern.ch.*

An extension of the original, **SHTTP** (**secure hypertext transfer protocol**) sets a standard for transmitting data safely over the Web. The more prevalent **SSL** (**secure sockets layer**) is designed to establish a secure connection between two computers.

hyper-

The over-and-above prefix meaning "excessive" and used excessively: *hypermedia, hyper-reality, hyperspeed.* If you use the prefix, don't believe the hype.

hypertext

A system of linking electronic documents. Click on a word or phrase, and you're taken to another page of information about that idea; click on a picture of a seductive jungle river, and you get info on how to travel there. Hypertext is reminiscent of the links between a footnote and the main body of your high school theme papers, except that connections rely on computer code rather than superscript numbers.

The concept of a hypertext information system may have first appeared in **"As We May Think,"** a 1945 essay by electrical engineer Vannevar Bush (see page 33). Twenty years later, Ted Nelson latched on to the dream of branching, nonlinear writing and spelled out his vision in *Literary Machines.* But it was **CERN** researcher Tim Berners-Lee who made the dream a reality by inventing HTTP, HTML, and URLs.

IBM

Founded by Herman Hollerith in 1896 as the Tabulating Machine Company and renamed in 1924, **International Business Machines** Corporation remains the largest computer company in the world. Its slogan: "Solutions for a Small Planet." Its nickname: Big Blue (also acceptable on first reference).

ICANN

The **Internet Corporation for Assigned Names and Numbers** is the nonprofit private group established in 1998 by the US government

to oversee the domain name system. Specifically, ICANN—which assumed the administrative functions once performed by **Network Solutions**—will open .com domain registration to competition by accrediting new registries (the first five are America Online, CORE, France Telecom, Melbourne IT, and Register.com). ICANN will also work with **WIPO** to hash out trademark policy and create new top-level domains (such as .shop, .arts, and .web) if needed. See **CORE**, **domain name**, **DNS**, **Network Solutions**.

icon

That trash can on your desktop, that pseudo-manila folder, that Bart Simpson cartoon. In other words, any small onscreen image—often a pictogram or visual metaphor—representing an application or document or directory in a graphical user interface.

IDG

The world's largest provider of high tech information services, **International Data Group** organizes conferences, publishes magazines, books, and Web sites, and offers industry analysis and consulting through its research subsidiary, International Data Corp. IDG is probably best known as the publisher of the innumerable . . . *for Dummies* books (350 titles and growing), which quickly expanded from a series teaching computer newbies to one helping novices of all kinds.

IEEE

Pronounced "eye-triple-E," the initials stand for the **Institute of Electrical and Electronics Engineers**, a leading standards body and the world's largest technical professional organization. The IEEE also sponsors conferences, symposia, and meetings across the globe and publishes more than 30 percent of the world's technical papers on electrical and computer engineering.

Officially created on January 1, 1963, the IEEE grew out of the American Institute of Electrical Engineers, which held its first exhibition back in October 1884, and the Institute of Radio

Engineers, a professional society and standards body that first met in May 1912.

IETF

The **Internet Engineering Task Force** is a self-organizing volunteer group that sets the protocol standards, creates the informational documents, and resolves various and sundry problems of the Internet. Members, divided into technical working groups, communicate through mailing lists and attend several meetings annually.

The unofficial IETF motto was coined by MIT professor Dave Clark: "We reject kings, presidents, and voting. We believe in rough consensus and running code."

ILEC

Pronounced "eye-leck." For more on the **incumbent local exchange carrier** scene, see **CLEC**.

IM

AOL converted millions of people with its **instant messenger**—the app of emails that announce themselves on your screen rather than waiting patiently in the inbox. One of those knows-no-boundaries emails is an **instant message**. The acronym instantly messaged itself into a verb, as in: *Hang on, I just got IMed,* or *I was IMing this guy last night and he . . .*

Sometimes styled **AIM**—for America Online's Instant Messenger—the service is so popular that Microsoft and Yahoo! introduced copycat versions, sparking an industry battle.

IMO

Online shorthand for **in my opinion**. Related terms include **IMHO** (in my humble opinion) and **IMNSHO** (in my not so humble opinion).

implementation

Used by engineers to refer to the physical or digital instantiation of an idea, rather than its abstract conception. As in *Microsoft's product plans involve great vision, though its implementation often falls short.* Used by non-engineers—far too often—to create clunky prose.

impression

In the world of online advertising, impressions or **ad views**—the number of times an ad is downloaded—are always good.

information superhighway

The whole digital enchilada—interactive, cable, broadband, 500-channel, into-your-home, and in-your-face. The American Dialect Society chose this as the new word of the year in 1993. But it was hardly "new" then: in 1978, then-Senator Al Gore Jr. introduced the term at a meeting of computer-industry folk, in homage to Senator Albert Gore Sr., his father. Gore père had helped establish the interstate highway system in the 1950s.

inkjet

There's no disputing the meaning of this adjective: it designates a "high-speed printing process in which jets of ink are broken up into electrostatically charged drops, which are guided by a computer program into positions that form printed characters on papers." (Thank you, *Webster's New World*, Third College Edition.)

But the style is all over the map: open, closed, hyphenated, and oddly capped. Blame the rampant confusion on various related trademarks, including DeskJet, Bubble Jet, and Laserjet. We stick with the *Wired* dictum "When in doubt, close it up."

Intel

The world's largest chip manufacturer, Intel Corporation dominates the CPU market with its hulking development, manufacturing, and marketing presence.

Despite bugs, antitrust investigations, and numerous patent-infringement skirmishes, Intel endures, pumping out more than 75 percent of all microprocessors worldwide.

No doubt, privacy watchdogs will remember 1999 as the year of the Pentium III **processor serial number**—essentially a Social Security number for a computer that allows corporations to recognize unidentified network users, track equipment, *and* monitor individuals. But tech hounds will remember it as the birth of **Itanium**, the first of the new IA-64 family of processors. With a 64-bit architecture that is twice as powerful as the Pentium III, Itanium is, well, no chip off the old block.

intellectual property

Often abbreviated as **IP**, this is legal jargon for "protected idea." IP covers patents, copyrights, and trademarks—all intangible, original assets that can be bought and sold.

The cut-and-paste ease of digital technology has heightened the IP debate, in which movie studios, record labels, and database companies scream the loudest.

They *cheered* the loudest, however, in 1998, when the **Digital Millennium Copyright Act** became law. It criminalizes efforts to circumvent technologies that restrict unauthorized copying. The law also makes it a crime to produce or sell any technology that can be used to break copyright protection. See **WIPO**.

internet

A network of connected networks. A generic term, often preceded by "an," which distinguishes it from the Internet.

Internet

In a 1962 paper titled "On-Line Man—Computer Communication," MIT professor J.C.R. Licklider—known as Lick—proposed an "intergalactic network," though he had no idea how to build it. "The hope," he wrote, "is that in not too many years, human brains and computing machines will be coupled . . . tightly, and that the resulting partnership will think as no human brain has ever thought and process data in a way not approached by the information-handling machines we know today."

Not long after, the Internet evolved from the small **Arpanet** into a worldwide network of computers communicating in a common language—TCP/IP—over telephone lines or microwave links. But the Net is more than that. It's a cultural watershed. It comprises the Web and an infinite number of newsgroups, chat rooms, and online forums. It is, as author Julian Dibbell says, "the single most complex information entity since the emergence of the human brain."

The name Internet derived from "internetting," Bob Taylor's term for connecting the multiple packet nets of the early '70s. Always initial capped, it is preceded by *the* unless being used as a modifier (as in *Internet service provider*). Don't say "on Internet." The **Net** (also initial capped) is synonymous with the Internet, though slightly more figurative.

Internet2

Launched in 1996, this broad effort to develop advanced network technologies and applications includes some 140 member universities and dozens of corporate partners. Sometimes styled **I2**. Sometimes derided as the irrelevant initiative of universities left behind by commercial networking technology.

Internet economy

Bigger than webonomics. Broader than the dot-com sector. The sum total of Net-enabled commerce, including retail sales, advertising and marketing, business-to-business commerce, the stock market, and any other economic exchange ushered in by the Internet.

Internet protocols

A jungle of initialisms that are never spelled out and nearly always capitalized: FTP, HTTP, POP, PPP, SMTP, TCP/IP.

Protocols are often stacked. On the Net, for instance, IP provides the basic service of creating and addressing packets of data. TCP runs on top of IP and acts as a traffic cop for reliably sending and receiving those blocks of data. The Web is essentially another layer in the protocol stack—HTTP—which specifies Web operations such as hyperlinking.

Internet service provider

An **ISP** jacks you in to the Net, lets you wander the Web, and may offer chat rooms, databases, or other entertainment or information areas. Major ISPs include America Online, AT&T WorldNet, MCI Worldcom, Netcom, PSINet, and UUNet Technologies.

Internet telephony

Net telephony (pronounced "tel-LEFF-ah-knee" and also known as **voice-over-IP**) turns the Internet into a telephone. You speak into the mike of your PC; your voice is digitized, compressed, and chopped into packets of data; your message zips through the modem and over phone lines to your sweetie's modem, which kicks the process into reverse.

While traditional telephone networks use dedicated circuits, with conversations speeding down private lines, Internet phone technology distributes words across public lines known as shared circuits.

Internet Phone and IPhone are trademarked by VocalTec Inc.; **I-phone** is sometimes the preferred generic noun for voice-over-IP.

Internet time

The accelerated speed of time in the digital world. A twist on the notion that every human year translates into seven dog years: one Internet year is the equivalent of seven years of analog existence.

InterNIC

A sort of Internet-related help desk, registrar, and phone book rolled into one. Through the '90s, the **Internet Network Information Center** and its national registry of domain names and owners was run by **Network Solutions, Inc.** (or **NSI**). That company's contract with the government ends in September 2000. See **domain name, ICANN, Network Solutions.**

intranet

A private network within an organization (always lowercase). Firewalls, machines that control access from the outside, often keep Internet traffic off an intranet. The seminal intranet was the newborn WWW—the network built to let scientists affiliated with CERN share internal documents and research. The term intranet first appeared on Usenet in January 1994, but it took another two years to really enter the lexicon—and the corporate world.

The related term **extranet**—coined by Ethernet inventor and Infoworld columnist Bob Metcalfe—designates a private network between organizations. An extranet might connect a manufacturer with its distributor or the distributor with its retail outlets.

IOW

Online shorthand for **in other words**, used by Net equivocators.

IP

Use the acronym, but if you must spell it out, use initial caps to differentiate **Internet Protocol** from a generic Internet protocol.

IP is the language that allows computers to communicate over the Internet, defining how data is cut up into packets and addressed in order to reach its destination. Every machine on a network is located and identified by its unique **IP address**—four sets of digits separated by periods (such as 206.221.206.188). The next generation **IPv6** will support longer addresses, if the networking community ever gets around to the upgrade.

The protocol often appears joined at the hip with transmission control protocol: **TCP/IP.**

IPO

The acronym for **initial public offering** refers to the first time shares of a private company are sold on the public market.

The new American Dream starts in a garage and ends in an IPO. Just look at Netscape, once the new economy's poster child, which the market valued at US$2.7 billion after one minute of trading.

Commonly used as a verb: *Mark my words—Oprah will IPO sooner or later.*

IRL

Online shorthand for life offline. It means **in real life.**

IRC

An international federation of Internet-connected computers, aligned in a client/server relationship. The **Internet Relay Chat** code was created by a Finn named Jarkko Oikarinen in 1988.

It's a stark ASCII world where anyone with Net access can go for free real-time chat, 24 hours a day.

If you want to spell it out, go ahead, but remember the initial caps. This at times improper netherworld is still a proper noun.

IS

The networking department of an organization. The ISers don't always agree about what the acronym stands for: some say **information systems**, others say **information services**. See also **MIS**.

ISDN

A set of digital telecommunications standards that transmits voice, video, and data over standard phone lines at up to 128 Kbps. Advertised as high-speed, low-cost Net access, **integrated services digital network** is an ugly duckling next to DSL and cable modems.

Its great promise, poor service, and expensive rates inspired the cracks "It Still Does Nothing" and "I Still Don't Know."

ISP

See **Internet service provider.**

IT

Now the single biggest part of the US economy, **information technology** accounts for about 11 percent of the GDP. Think tools for creating, sorting, storing, and moving data.

Java

One-size-fits-all software, in the words of its inventor James Gosling. A multiplatform, object-oriented language developed by Sun for use over distributed networks like the Internet. Conceived in 1990 and released in December 1995, Java promised to supercharge the Web with animations and real-time interactivity. In reality, it supercharged only ad banners and set off a technolegal battle between Sun and Microsoft.

JavaScript

The scripting language—designed to run inside Web pages—shares only the name with Sun's Java. Developed by Netscape's

Brendan Eich, who christened it LiveScript, the program was renamed by marketers hoping to ride the Java wave. In fact, JavaScript far outdid Sun's language—nearly 10 percent of all Web pages contain its code, which can, for example, identify the computer, browser, and plug-ins used by a visitor and present the appropriate interface.

JPEG

Use the acronym, pronounced "jay-peg," which usually refers to the standard method of **lossy compression** for photographs, created by the professional organization with the same name: **Joint Photographic Experts Group**. The technology breaks down an image into a grid and uses a fairly basic mathematical formula to simplify the visual information in each square. This reduces the space needed to store the image, but degrades the quality, often making it look blocky.

K

You already know this informal shorthand for *kilo*, or *thousand* (as in dollars): *He's pulling in 500K a year*. But it might just as easily stand in for **kilobytes**: *I'll zap you the JPEGs but the message file will be 900K*.

If you're talking kilobits or kilobits per second, use the shorthand *Kb* or *Kbps*, and note the lowercase *b*.

kernel

The nucleus of an operating system, the kernel provides basic services to other parts of the OS, assigns processing time and priority to various programs, and manages address spaces in memory and storage. By contrast, the **shell** of an OS interacts with user commands.

key

Talking hardware, a key is what your fingers dance on. Talking cryptography, keys encode and decode messages. Longer keys, containing more bits, are more difficult to crack and therefore provide stronger protection.

key escrow

Uncle Sam's favorite encryption scheme, which raised its devilish head in 1993 as the Clipper Chip and was euphemistically rechristened **key recovery** or **key management** after that chip hit the fan. Adopting this method, users would agree to store, or "escrow," their private keys in a repository controlled by a third party. Many corporations use key escrow to make sure they have access to their data if an employee suddenly leaves the company; the FBI would like to make key escrow systems mandatory for anyone using strong crypto. The Feds have yet to find any takers, but until they give up trying, don't hyphenate the adjective: *key escrow encryption.*

killer app

The Holy Grail of the digital age (and just as much of a cliché). The software application that breathes life into an underused technology. The first killer app—Lotus 1-2-3—drove the nascent PC market, just as VisiCalc did for the Apple II. Since then, however, the term has become more fanfare than fact. The Newton was gonna be a killer app, and so was interactive TV. Then it was Sun's Java. The term has become so shopworn that funnyman Gary Trudeau and filmmaker Robert Altman titled their Silicon Valley TV spoof *Killer App.*

kluge

In common usage, this noun refers to an inelegant solution and rhymes with "stooge." In the US, it's often confused with *kludge,* derived from the Scottish (and, later, British military) slang for toilet. Spelled correctly, kluge is a subversion of the German word *klug* (clever). Use the adjective **klugey** when you want to dis a product.

(Visit the Jargon File—*www.ccil.org/jargon*—or its book version, *The New Hacker's Dictionary*, for a less klugey explanation.)

LAN

A network of computers centered in a physical location. The fantastic names for the various kinds of **local-area networks**—

FireWired, token ring (or IBM's proprietary Token Ring), and Ethernet—make up for the dullness of the acronym, which is pronounced "lan."

The alpha geek responsible for the office network is, according to Jargon Watch-er Gareth Branwyn, the **LANlord.**

landline

The soon-to-be-quaint telco term refers to the traditional twisted copper pair phone line that connects your telephone (cordless or no) to the local substation.

Lara Croft

The Sharon Stone of video gaming. Well-endowed and heavily armed, the hero of *Tomb Raider* has become a cult figure, with a television show, a movie, and a bevy of action figures.

the last mile

A metaphor for local loop—the final stretch of wiring that connects a house or neighborhood to the larger regional telecom network. Most of the lines crisscrossing the country are high-capacity fiber-optic, while the local loop is limited-bandwidth copper. The last mile, then, is the bandwidth bottleneck. Copper's too wimpy, fiber's too expensive, and the first telco or ISP to solve the last mile problem will win the broadband race.

"Only the telephone companies could have come up with a phrase like 'the last mile,'" notes Steve G. Steinberg. "It requires the kind of self-importance fostered by years without competition to assume you are the center of the universe—that the customer represents the last mile."

LAT

Online shorthand for **lovely and talented**. A CompuServish compliment.

LCD

The primitive, two-tone screen of a digital watch, a pager, or a vintage computer is a **liquid crystal display**. Do not write "LCD display."

leased line

A line of one's own. Also known as a **dedicated line**. The exclusive 24/7 phone line required for a high-speed data connection. Rent the leased line, buy the T-1 service, and you're ready to network.

LED

The tiny butlers of electronics: **light-emitting diodes** are the little red, green, or yellow lights on older equipment.

LEO

Just 500 to 1,000 miles into the heavens, **low Earth orbit** is the home of planned Dick Tracy–like global satellite networks such as Iridium and Teledesic (not to mention a few surveillance operations). LEO satellites greatly expand the reach of wireless communications, offering two-way paging and email, but until the US$3-a-minute cost of service comes down, companies launching their birds into low Earth orbit might as well be shooting for the moon. Iridium, for its part, has already filed for bankruptcy.

Lexis-Nexis

Lexis, the largest legal research database in the US, was developed in 1973 by paper giant Mead Data Central and sold in 1994 to publishing giant Reed Elsevier, Inc. The Nexis half dates to 1979 and holds news articles from some 18,000 news and business publications. The database is too expensive for the masses, but de rigueur in libraries, universities, and newsrooms.

link

As a verb, to attach computers via a network, or documents through hypertext. As a noun, a hypertext jump or connection between files. **Link rot** refers to that irritating phenomenon of Web searching: the dead end you hit when a page has been deleted or moved.

Linux

The little operating system that could, Linux (pronounced "linn-ucks") turns your PC into a workstation. From a 1990 do-it-yourself project started by Finnish college student Linus Torvalds, Linux has grown into a full-featured, very stable

Unix-like operating system, codeveloped and maintained as freeware by an international cadre of hackers. It is also preinstalled alongside Windows by IBM, HP, and Dell Computer. Having outcompeted several commercial offerings, Linux is the preferred platform for small Internet servers.

Eric S. Raymond on Linux: "Possibly the purest crystallization of the Hacker Ethic to date, and a remarkable demonstration of the Net's ability to host new forms of creative collaboration."

Lisp

Developed by John McCarthy in the late 1950s, **List Processing** has long been the dominant language of AI research—and not much else.

listserv

Capitalized, Listserv is the trademarked name for software that manages electronic mailing lists. But the name has become so ubiquitous (Listserv and the similar Majordomo control 75 percent of the market) that many treat it as a generic term, as in *She has been the subject of ridicule on countless newsgroups and listservs.*

A Swedish programmer named Eric Thomas wrote Listserv, the first mailing list software, in 1986. L-Soft International bought the license and trademarked the name in 1994, but by that time the word had been used in vernacular by computer geeks, technology trade journalists, and electronic list subscribers for years.

Note that the final *e* is missing. That's because program names on older IBM mainframes and machines running Unix were limited to eight characters.

log on

To access a computer or network. When you're done, you **log off**. The verb must stay detached from the preposition—after all, would the verb survive in the past tense as logoned or logged-on? The gerund would be a spelling train wreck: loggingon.

The synonyms **log in** and **log out** are more common in the Unix world.

Keep the *to* discrete—don't write "log onto" or "log into." Unconvinced by our prepositional logic? Consider the difference between *He came on to me* and *He came onto me.*

login

The account name used to gain access to a network, server, Web site, or other computer system. In addition to a login, registered users have a password.

logon

The procedure to gain access to a network. Its partner: **logoff**. Also an adjective: *Some boards offer 20 minutes a day of free logon time.*

LOL

This shorthand for **laughing out loud** is big on AOL.

Luddites

The original Luddites—named after legendary leader Ned Ludd—were members of a radical agrarian movement that surfaced in Nottinghamshire, England, in the early 19th century. As textile workers, the Luddites violently opposed the machines in factories and mills that ushered in not only the Industrial Revolution but also the workers' own economic demise.

In the 20th century, Luddite has become the pat put-down for anyone opposed to technology. Note Microsoft lawyer John Warden's claim that the US Justice Department's antitrust suit against the company marked a "return of the Luddites." Some technocritics, though, are proud to call themselves **neo-Luddites**.

lurk

To hang out in an online conference or forum without copping to it by saying—er, writing—anything. The related noun **lurkers** is a synonym for the silent majority of cyberspace.

Lynx

A word-y Web browser, used almost exclusively by hackers, engineers, and scientists who hate graphics-heavy interfaces and prefer speed to spectacle. Talking browsers for the visually impaired are based on this text-only program.

Macintosh

Created at Apple Computer by Jef Raskin—who named the computer for his favorite kind of apple—the Macintosh was introduced in January 1984. It popularized the GUI (originally developed at Xerox PARC and SRI International) with its windows and menubars. And it made the desktop—not to mention the mouse—a staple of computing. Often called simply **Mac.**

"Very few tools transform their culture," wrote Steven Levy in *Insanely Great: The Life and Times of Macintosh, the Computer That Changed Everything.* "Before 1984, the concept of regular human beings participating in digital worlds belonged to the arcane realm of data processing and science fiction. Long after its departure, the Macintosh will be remembered as the product that brought just plain people, uninterested in the particulars of technology, into the trenches of the information age—and that did it with an unforgettable artistic flourish."

See **operating system** for Umberto Eco's description of Macintosh true believers.

macro-

Long, great, or even excessive: *macrobiotics, macroeconomics.*

macro

In tech talk, macro often stands alone as an adjective (*we need to think in macro terms*) and as a noun is short for **macroinstruction**, where a single command or keystroke represents a set of more complicated instructions.

MAE

A peering point where the big ISPs and network backbones converge and trade packets. Owned by MCI WorldCom, pronounced like the month, and short for **metropolitan area exchange**, the MAEs resemble the cloverleafs where interstates converge. The two largest are MAE East and, our favorite, MAE West, which gives new meaning to the phrase "Why don't you come up and see me sometime?" See **NAP**.

mailbomb

Not an analog explosive device, but rather a sustained avalanche of emails sent to one or more users on a network to overwhelm the receiving node until it crashes. Often sent in retaliation for netiquette violations. Also a verb, meaning "to send a mailbomb."

Being mailbombed, like being spammed, involves receiving unwanted email, but the two are not synonymous. See **spam**.

mailing list

An ongoing email discussion devoted to specific topics, ranging from the polemical to the pedantic to the purely entertaining: Voters Telecommunications Watch, Interesting People, the Drudge Report. The first wide-distribution Internet mailing list is still around: SF-Lovers, for science fiction fans.

A mailing list is technically an email address that uses a **mail exploder** to redirect a message to a list of addresses. Mailing lists may be public or private. They may be edited by a list moderator; they may be an unfiltered stream of messages from participants. (Although mailing lists are associated with Usenet, they originated on early UUCP and Arpanet connections.)

mailto:

The HTML tag that identifies a text string as an email address and links it to a browser's mail program.

mainframe

Big iron. Originally, the "main frame" referred to the metal or plastic husk that held the central processing unit of a room-size computer. When refrigerator-size **minicomputers** were developed in the '70s, the older machines became known as "mainframe computers," a term soon shortened to "mainframes" and roughly synonymous with "dinosaurs." A principal victim of the '80s PC revolution.

majordomo

Like the similar listserv program, this mailing-list freeware is often used generically, without the capital *M.* The word often appears in the address header of a mailing list, like this one covering high tech news and events:

To: ip-sub-1 @majordomo.pobox.com
Subject: IP: Demise of BYTE

the matrix

The vast computer network in William Gibson's 1984 novel *Neuromancer*. As the Net developed, the term was also used to describe the growing mass of interconnected networks. Gibson's coinage was adopted as the title of the 1999 cyberthriller movie starring Keanu Reeves.

Mbone

Pronounced "em-bone," and short for **multicast backbone**, this Internet test bed was invented at Xerox PARC. The high-bandwidth technology adds video and audio dimensions to online communications. The spread of IP multicast technologies, though, has been hampered by bandwidth bottlenecks.

MCI WorldCom

The goliath of long distance, created when WorldCom ate MCI—straight off of British Telecom's plate—in 1998. MCI WorldCom, Inc. is now the Number Two telco.

Some history: MCI entered the big time in 1972, when the FCC granted the company a long-distance license, putting it in direct competition with AT&T.

Some etymology: MCI illustrates how thoroughly initialisms are accepted in the telecom industry. It briefly stood for Microwave Communications, Inc.

McLuhan, Marshall

By the time of his death in 1980, Marshall McLuhan had been dismissed by respectable academics and was known in the popular press as an eccentric intellectual whose day in the media spotlight had come and gone. But in the whirl of the Digital Revolution, McLuhan became the electronic culture's immortal saint, with his epistles *The Gutenberg Galaxy*, *Understanding Media*, and *The Medium is the Massage*. " 'The medium is the message' and 'the global village' are recited like mantras," writes Gary Wolf, "despite the fact that hardly anyone who quotes McLuhan has read his books."

While media critics canonize the man, *New Yorker* writer John Seabrook verbified him, writing in a book review that a young author "resists the temptation to McLuhanize about virtual reality, space, and time, and what it all means."

measurements

Using only the US Customary system of weights and measurements (also known as the inch-pound system) is a sure sign of American myopia. Use metrics when that is the measurement system of the place you're writing about: *The Austro-Czech performance artist Karel Dudesek once mailed himself 500 kilometers across Germany in a crate to take part in an art competition.*

meatspace

Where you are as you read this book. Not cyberspace.

media and medium

Once upon an analog time, these two were just the singular and plural nouns derived from the Latin for "middle." No more. In the digital age, **medium** and **media** are used in quite different contexts:

medium—the catchall phrase for any physical material used to store data, such as DVD, disk, tape, or paper. The plural in this case would be **media**, since **mediums** are those who claim to chat with spirits of the dead.
media—synonymous, especially among vague and lazy writers, with *the press*. We prefer specific terms like *print journalism*, *TV*, *radio*, *the Internet*, or *the Web* when referring to what *Webster's* calls "the agencies of mass communication." Media in this context is becoming less and less plural in concept and can take a singular verb: *Today's media is tomorrow's fossil fuel.*
mass media—any means of communication intended to reach millions of people at once. This term encompasses newspapers, magazines, radio, television, motion pictures, and the Internet. Mass media no longer requires a plural verb: *Mass media is obsolete; niche media is in.*

new media is one of many terms—including **interactive media** and **multimedia**—that are used to refer to works existing in a digital format. Like **old media**, the compound noun takes a singular verb.

Media Lab

Founded by Nicholas Negroponte in 1985, the MIT Media Lab is a corporate-funded hub of research. Devoted to the study of new technologies, the lab is concerned with developing innovative prototypes rather than viable commercial products.

The Medium is the Massage

Published in 1967, this well-designed volume of McLuhanisms was one of the media scholar's few bestsellers. Style fussbudgets lowercase the *i* in *is*; this is how the verb appeared on the book's cover.

What is Marshall McLuhan's message? "All media work us over completely. They are so pervasive in their personal, political, economic, aesthetic, psychological, moral, ethical, and social consequences that they leave no part of us untouched, unaffected, unaltered. The medium is the massage. Any understanding of social and cultural change is impossible without a knowledge of the way media work as environments. All media are extensions of some human faculty—psychic or physical."

the medium is the message

Today this McLuhanism, which is just one of the eccentric media critic's catchy slogans, is both a commandment and a cliché, often quoted and often misunderstood. Marshall McLuhan believed that the form of media (print or television) had a far greater transformative effect on society than the content (ideas and images).

mega-

A variation of *megalo-*, meaning large, great, or grand. Mega- can also mean simply enormous, as in *megatruck* or *megatrend.* On occasion we let it stand alone—especially when it's modifying a polysyllabic noun: *mega* corporation.

"Mega is a realm that abolishes the squalid everyday limits of lesser beings," muses Bruce Sterling in *Wired*. Megaprojects "are not big simply for functional reasons. They are not about the bottom line. Megaprojects are about the top line—the transcendent, the beautiful, and the sublime. They are built for the purpose of inspiring sheer, heart-thumping awe."

meg(s)

Slang for **megabyte(s)**: *Is the new Internet Explorer worth the 54-meg download?*

meme

Contagious idea. Thought virus. Unit of cultural inheritance. Rhymes with scheme.

Evolutionary biologist Richard Dawkins introduced the word (though not the idea) in *The Selfish Gene*. His meaning: an idea that functions in the mind the same way a gene functions in the body. An especially infectious idea is a **viral meme**.

MEMS

Lilliputian mechanical systems, meaning **micro-electrical-mechanical systems** and pronounced "memz," that can sense heat, light, motion, and sound. Attach a MEMS sensor to a microchip and—presto!—it'll tell your Honda's air bag to inflate when it detects a sudden deceleration. Or it'll conduct the simple analysis for a home blood-pressure kit.

The new darling of folks who once championed nanotech, MEMS technology promises to be the greatest technological advance since the transistor. But it's not there yet.

menubar

The rectangular bar of pulldown tools and commands featured in any graphical user interface.

menu-driven

The opposite of **command-line**. Since menu-driven interfaces are the norm these days, this clunky compound can often be driven off the page.

meta

From the Greek for *after, among,* or *beyond*, the term suggests "the big picture." A *metalanguage* is a language used to describe another language. In an academic context, the term designates a field of study that critiques or builds on an older one: *metaphysics, metalinguistics.* In the Web context, a **meta tag** defines the contents of a page so that it can be indexed by search engines. Colloquially, the noun can stand alone, as in *Let's get meta,* meaning "Let's look at the big picture."

metaverse

Coined by Neal Stephenson in *Snow Crash:* "So Hiro's not actually here at at all. He's in a computer-generated universe that his computer is drawing onto his goggles and pumping into his earphones. In the lingo, this imaginary place is known as the Metaverse."

Lose the initial cap. (No offense, Neal.)

micro-

From the prefix denoting one-millionth, used to mean "minute" or "tiny": *microcomputer, micromanagement.*

microserf

Douglas Coupland is responsible for this one: he created the term to describe the young coders who slave away for Bill Gates on the Redmond supercampus. We've let the noun become generic (i.e., no initial cap).

Microsoft

The software giant founded by Bill Gates and Paul Allen in 1975 and led today by Gates and President Steve Ballmer. In 1980, when IBM needed software for its new personal computer, Gates hustled out and bought DOS from Tim Patterson, another Seattle programmer. Today Microsoft is legendary for its single-minded focus and ability to leverage—with a crowbar if necessary—its dominance of the desktop PC market.

Formally the Microsoft Corporation and based in Redmond, Washington, the company has picked up many monikers: Big

Brother, the Evil Empire, the Lord of Lock-in, Microsquish, Microsloth, and—on Wall Street—Mister Softie (for MSFT).

MIDI

Pronounced "mid-dee," the **musical instrument digital interface** is the protocol that allows a computer, a synthesizer, a musical keyboard, and recording equipment to communicate. Think of it as a LAN for musicians.

MIME

This email extension standard lets users send audio, graphics, and video files in an email message. Developed by Nathaniel Borenstein at Carnegie Mellon during the '80s, **multipurpose Internet mail extensions** replaced the earlier **uuencode** technique for encoding binary data in email.

Avoid the redundant "Internet MIME." We pronounce it as we would the mute performer, but use all caps, because this is how it appears in email.

mindshare

A buzzword for "brand awareness." This contrasts with **market share**. If market share is what people are spending their money on, mindshare is what's on their lips. But mind your mindshares—"when a salesman says 'I'm building mindshare,'" notes Po Bronson, "he means he hasn't sold a thing."

mips

This measure of computer processing speed—**millions of instructions per second**—is sometimes derided by hackers who say the acronym stands for "meaningless indication of processor speed." It rhymes with "lips" and, like other measurements (bps, mph), should be lowercase: *He's got lots of mips but no I/O.*

Note: MIPS Technologies, Inc. manufactures microprocessors.

mirroring

The automatic duplication of data from one disk to another as a form of network backup (if one disk becomes damaged, the other can continue working). Related words include the noun **mirror site**—it helps distribute the network traffic load.

MIS

A stand-in for **management information systems**, it refers to the folks who keep the office clients and servers and local-area networks working. Also **IS.**

modem

Pronounced "mow-dem," this device was once long-windedly called a *modulator/demodulator*. Broadly, it is a piece of hardware that allows computers to talk to each other, by translating digital information into analog signals that can be sent over regular phone lines and redigitized at the receiving end. At times it helps to be specific about the magic box: *56K modem, cable modem, fax modem.* "DSL modem," mind you, is a misuse of the term—that *digital* protocol needs no analog translator.

In 1960, AT&T built into its Data-phone the first modem, which was designed to transmit data across the Bell Systems network. The first commercial modems appeared in the late 1960s, running at 110 baud. Then came the 300- and 1200-baud devices, then 9600 bps boxes, then the slew of kbps wonders: 14.4s, 28.8s, and 56.6s.

MOO

Meaning **MUD, object-oriented**, this term is pronounced like the cow's call. An online role-playing game in the MUD family (see **MUD**), it is based on object-oriented technology. LambdaMOO, one of the best known, was launched as an experiment by Xerox PARC researcher Pavel Curtis in 1991.

Beware the habit of writing *MUDs and MOOs* when *MUDs* alone would and should suffice. MOO, after all, is a subset of the general category of MUDs and is therefore implied in that acronym. Using the phrase *MUDs and MOOs* is analogous to writing *birds and ducks.*

Moore's Law

In 1965, Intel cofounder Gordon Moore stated that the number of transistors we can fit on a chip—and, therefore, its potential power—will double every 18 months, while the cost of making chips will fall by 50 percent. Although it's more self-fulfilling prophecy than natural law, his assertion has become accepted wisdom in the high tech industry.

"These days," notes Stewart Brand, "Moore's Law is treated as a general statement that computers get drastically better every year—faster, cheaper, smaller—and that this will occur indefinitely." Moore himself, however, predicts it will hold only "for a few more generations of technology."

Moore's Second Law—not coined by Moore—predicts that the capital investment required to build each new generation of chips will increase until no company can afford to build a new chip fab.

MorF

Short for **male or female**, this is the common online response to a posting by alex, chris, or another gender-unspecific name.

morph

A verb meaning to turn from one thing into another, **morph** evolved from *metamorphosis*. It describes the double process of warping and color-blending two images or 3-D objects so that one melds smoothly into the other.

The gerund, **morphing**, refers to computer-generated special-effects techniques (it's what made Jim Carrey become The Mask and what turned Robert Patrick's evil cyborg into liquid metal in *Terminator 2*).

Mosaic

The mother of all Web browsers. NCSA Mosaic introduced untold numbers of novices to the Web in 1993. Created at the University of Illinois at Urbana-Champaign by the 23-year-old Marc Andreessen, Mosaic allowed users to travel through the world of electronic information using a point-and-click interface. Netscape Communications Corporation, founded by Andreessen and Jim Clark in 1994, was the most successful early attempt to commercialize Mosaic. See **browser**, **NCSA**, **Netscape**.

motherboard

The main circuit board of a computer, containing the CPU and other dominant components. The **daughterboard** is a computer logic board that plugs into the motherboard and offers supplementary functions such as video capture and 3-D graphics enhancement.

motion-capture

An f/x magic trick and the digital version of the man-in-the-suit. Put motion sensors on an actor, track his movements, and apply his biomechanics to an animated character, CG beast, or even a virtual human and you've done motion-capture. Or "mocap," as they quip in the industry. Think of the extras in *Titanic*.

mouse

Invented in 1964 by Douglas Engelbart, the mouse remains the most common computer navigational device.

If you want to see copy editors at their best (er, worst?), poll them on the plural of **mouse**. Most avoid it as if it were a diseased rodent. (*The Microsoft Manual of Style for Technical Publications* suggests the wimpy "mouse devices.") While some favor continuing the mousy metaphor into the plural with "mice" (à la *The New York Times*), others argue that the computer appendage is distinguished from the animal and should follow the most common method of pluralization (adding *-s* or *-es*), just as *louse* becomes *louses* when it defines a group of cranky editors. Put us among the louses; we prefer *mouses*.

When asked for the definitive answer, Engelbart himself demurred, saying he hadn't "given the matter much thought." Nor could his colleagues remember who first nicknamed the device, though all agree that the cord or "tail" initially came out the back. "Very soon we realized that the connecting wire should be brought out the front instead of the back," Engelbart notes, but by then the name had stuck.

BTW: **mouseclick** refers to the way mouses communicate with computers, **mousepad** is the mouse's turf, and **mouseover** is what happens when simply moving the cursor over an element on a Web page triggers some change, like the appearance of a menu or a small animation.

MP3

A digital audio file format with CD quality that lets Internet users download songs to a PC or to a portable player like the Rio. Developed in 1991 by researchers at the Fraunhofer Institute in Germany, the technology (whose full name is **MPEG-1, layer 3**) terrifies the music industry. But it titillates consumers, who are flocking to MP3.com to download songs by the hundreds of thousands.

Competing technologies include the AT&T format A2B, LiquidAudio, and the **SDMI** standard, named for the **Secure Digital Music Initiative** that is developing it.

MPEG

Pronounced "em-peg," this video and audio compression standard is named after the professional organization that created it—the **Moving Picture Experts Group.** (The acronym can also stand for the society itself.)

MSN

The creation of the **Microsoft Network** marked the first salvo in Bill Gates's battle to take over the Internet. Launched in August 1995, the online service never left AOL eating its bits, as promised. However, backed by Bill's assets (not to mention his ambition), MSN has launched some successful sites—such as *Slate* and the travel resource Expedia—and teamed with the TV broadcast veteran to create MSNBC.

Mtops

Standing for **million theoretical operations per second** and pronounced "muh-tops," it's a measurement of the number of operations a computer can perform in the snap of a finger. It is also a measure of export law: currently, computers performing more than 6,500 Mtops cannot be exported to China, Russia, India, or any country still developing nuclear arms.

MUD

A **multi-user dungeon.** Or **multi-user domain.** Or **multi-user dimension.** (*Wired* generally spells *multiuser* solid, but in this case the acronym makes more sense if you keep the hyphen. Wiser yet to just use **MUD.**)

A type of online role-playing game that provides participants a shared virtual space, MUDs are about social interaction. They derive their name from Dungeons & Dragons, the face-to-face role-playing game that swept adolescent boyhood in the early 1970s. A MUD is a virtual space, accessible via the Internet, where players create identities, participating in a new kind of virtual parlor game.

The term MUD encompasses many kinds of multiuser environments, including MOOs, MUSHes, MUCKs, MUSEs, and TinyMUDs. MUD may also be a verb, whose gerund is **MUDding**. People who MUD are **MUDders**.

multi-

The combining form of the word multiple: *multitasking, multiuser, multithreading*.

multicasting

A term with multimeanings. On the Internet, a bandwidth-saving trick of broadcasting data packets that can be received by multiple people. In telecom circles, squeezing multiple signals or data streams into a single spectrum channel. In this context, multicast is synonymous with "multichannel" or "multiplex."

multimedia

A vague term used for anything that combines text, sound, graphics, video, and interactivity. Sueann Ambron coined the word when she founded Apple's seminal (and now defunct) Multimedia Lab, though others at Apple preferred "hypermedia."

multitasking

Doing more than one thing at a time. Originally, the word referred to a computer running two or more programs simultaneously. Nowadays, multitasking can apply to humans who, say, talk on the phone, read email, and eat lunch at the same time.

Myst

In 1993, Broderbund Software released *Myst,* the first CD-ROM smash hit. Its creators, brothers Robyn and Rand Miller, designed a kind of puzzle inside a novel inside a painting—only with music. *Myst* did more than set a new standard for graphics. As writer Jon Carroll once described: "It was beautiful, complicated, emotional, dark, intelligent, and absorbing. *Myst* was the only thing like itself; it had invented its own category."

nano-

Technically represents one-billionth. Deriving from the Greek *nanos*, or dwarf, the combining form means smaller than small: *nanotube, nanobuck*. The latter, literally, is one ten-millionth of a penny, though the word is more valuable as a metaphor for the microtransactions that weboconomists expect will dominate the Internet economy.

As a noun, **nano** is common shorthand for **nanotechnology**, the research and development of molecular robots.

NAP

Pronounced like the short bit of sleep, the acronym is networking lingo for **network access point** or **provider**. Think of NAPs as the major joints of the Internet—where the large backbones connect. Originally operated by the National Science Foundation, these network connectors are run by major telcos like Sprint and MCI WorldCom. See **MAE**.

Nasdaq

Pronounced "naz-dack," it should be initial capped. A distributed Wall Street, the **National Association of Securities Dealers Automated Quotations** was established in 1971, and has grown to become the second-largest stock market in the US (after the New York Stock Exchange). The national computer network revolutionized the over-the-counter market, while becoming home to high tech stocks like those of Apple, MCI, and Intel. Nasdaq merged with the shrinking American Stock Exchange in 1998.

NCSA

After releasing NCSA Mosaic to the world in August 1993, the **National Center for Supercomputing Applications** at the University of Illinois at Urbana-Champaign was pillaged: in April 1994, Jim Clark wooed several key developers away to launch Mosaic Communications, which soon became the celebrated Netscape

Communications Corporation. NCSA still exists, as telnetters well know, though it has yet to produce another Mosaic.

NDA

The **nondisclosure agreement** is a "mum's the word" contract that companies often require outsiders to sign before they will unveil or discuss projects in development. Colloquially, the acronym refers to a state of suspended animation: *I'm under NDA*. It's also used as a verb: *Sorry, but I'm NDA'd on that.*

nerd

A brainy person enamored of technology. The moniker is considered a badge of honor.

Word nerds trace the term to *If I Ran the Zoo*, a 1950 story by Dr. Seuss—"And then, just to show them, I'll sail to Ka-Troo / And Bring Back an It-Kutch, a Preep, and a Proo / A Nerkle, a Nerd, and a Seersucker, too!" But it was TV's *Happy Days* that took *nerd* prime-time: the Fonz and friends used the epithet to refer to any socially awkward, uncool person.

Douglas Coupland describes the '90s type in *Microserfs:* "At 2:30 A.M., the Safeway was completely empty save for us and a few other Microsoft people just like us—hair-trigger geeks in pursuit of just the right snack. Nerds get what they want when they want it, and they go psycho if it's not immediately available. Nerds over-focus. I guess that's the problem. But it's precisely this ability to narrow-focus that makes them so good at code writing: one line at a time, one line in a strand of millions."

Net

The world of cyberspace. The abbreviation for the Internet. The initial cap differentiates the Net (note the definite article) from any old computer network or, for that matter, a measure of profit, a tennis court divider, or a piece of fishing equipment.

net.

Pronounced "net-dot." Once the prefix of choice to indicate the people, places, and events in cyberspace, it pays homage to the flat organization of early Usenet days, when groups were named net.singles, net.suicide, net.etc. But in a 1987 reorganization grandiloquently called the Great Renaming—"as if it were a Vatican synod or a constitutional convention," notes Andrew Leonard—Usenet's ever-burgeoning newsgroups were reorganized into hierarchies with descriptive names: biz., rec., soc., news., sci., comp., talk., and alt.

Cyber scrits held sentimentally to the prefix long after '87 to give us net.goddesses, net.public, net.parties, net.outcry, and, of course, net.sex. Only recently has the cliché been traded in for *.com* and *e-*.

netiquette

The do's and don'ts of the cyberworld, the need for which was described by Virginia Shea in her 1996 book, *Netiquette:* "The Net right now is a little like New York in the late 19th century—waves of immigrants imposing themselves upon an established society. Not surprisingly, the newcomers don't always behave according to local custom, and members of the old society are sometimes suspicious and resentful."

netizen

A member of the Net community, especially an active participant or member of a Web site or Usenet group.

Netscape

The new economy's corporate poster child. (See **Mosaic** for history.) Netscape can refer either to software like the Netscape Navigator Web browser or to Netscape Communications Corporation, the company that cashed in on the Web with a legendary IPO in August 1995, fought Microsoft in the browser wars, and sold its soul to AOL in 1998.

The noun is invoked generically by Guy Kawasaki types who use **netscape** as a reflexive verb meaning to be unfairly slaughtered by Microsoft: *We were netscaped when they started giving away the software.*

network computer

A dumb box connected to a smart network and also called an **NC.** Larry Ellison, founder of Oracle and nemesis of Bill Gates, vowed these less-than-US$500 machines would bring the fall of the PC (and Microsoft with it). Right.

Network Solutions

The Internet's ex-landlord. In 1993, the National Science Foundation granted the Herndon, Virginia-based company the exclusive right to register all .com, .org, and .net domain names. As the Net grew, Network Solutions, Inc. earned millions of dollars and almost as many critics, who decried its monopolistic practices and ham-handed procedures for resolving domain name disputes. The company compressed its name to **NSI** in 1999, the same year its monopoly ended. See **ICANN, DNS, domain name**.

neural net

Silicon network built to emulate neurological and biological systems and an important area of AI research. Software agents, for instance, use neural networks to compare an individual's interests to the larger system of rules and behaviors.

Neuromancer

William Gibson's science fiction classic and a cyberpunk bible. Published in 1984, this futuristic thriller enriched the modern lexicon with the slang of the Japanese yakuza, as well as words such as *the matrix* and, of course, the new medium's ur-word, *cyberspace:* "He still dreamed of cyberspace, hope fading nightly. All the speed he took, all the turns he'd taken and the corners he'd cut in Night City, and still he'd see the matrix in his sleep, bright lattices of logic unfolding across the colorless void."

the new economy

The digital economy. The information economy. *Not* the industrial economy.

As Kevin Kelly writes in *New Rules for the New Economy:* "It is global. It favors intangible things—ideas, information, and relationships. And it is intensely interlinked. These three attributes produce a new type of marketplace and society, one that is rooted in ubiquitous electronic networks."

Believers in the new economy repeat the law of increasing returns and the law of plenitude, recognize the power of network externalities and decentralized systems, and value relationships over productivity. Do you buy it?

newbie

Pronounced "noo-bee," the condescending term for a Net neophyte derives from "new being." The noun was popularized by Usenet, although *The New Hacker's Dictionary* traces it back to the British public schools and military. Newbies tend to be distinguished by their cluelessness about netiquette.

NIH

Short for **not invented here**, the acronym is heard from MIT to Microsoft. It's a term of derision for the hubris of others and is never self-applied: *They tried to write their own OS instead of using Linux? They have a real NIH problem.*

NII

Al Gore first imagined the **National Information Infrastructure**, a nationwide network that would be part of a larger **Global Information Infrastructure** (**GII**). Typical Gorespeak, the term didn't really sing. The Net is still the Net, while the NII is, well, a not.

1984

Darkly futuristic novel by George Orwell published in 1949. Its title has become a synonym for a stark, cold, authoritarian soci ety. The indelible Apple television commercial introducing the Macintosh (it only ran once and people are still talking about it) alluded to Orwell—"Why 1984 won't be like *1984*."

NIST

Properly, the agency is called the **National Institute of Standards and Technology**, but the acronym is used without an article and pronounced "nist." Formerly called the National Bureau of Standards, NIST is the division of the Commerce Department charged with promoting official computer industry standards, and with touting high tech development to spur economic growth. Counting its previous incarnation, the agency has been around since 1901.

node

Also called a **host**. A device—a computer, printer, modem, or server—connected to a network to which data can be addressed.

nontrivial

Significant or impressive. An adjective of ironic understatement, as in this programmer's compliment on a piece of code: *That's a nontrivial accomplishment.* Also used by suits: *We're talking nontrivial amounts of money.*

NSA

Created by President Harry Truman in 1952, the **National Security Agency** is the intelligence body within the US Department of Defense devoted to the causes of spooks. It is also the center for the government's study of cryptology. The high tech industry has been pitted against the NSA since Whitfield Diffie and Martin Hellman developed public key cryptography in 1976. See **Clipper Chip**, **cryptography**.

NSF

Spell out the **National Science Foundation** on first reference, using NSF in subsequent references. A national funding organization, the NSF operated **NSFNet**—the backbone of the Internet until 1995.

NSP

A **network service provider** is an ISP for ISPs. These Internet wholesalers, such as MCI WorldCom or Sprint, run parts of the network backbone and resell connectivity to smaller service providers.

NTSC

While the FCC decides who does what with the spectrum, the **National Television Standards Committee** controls *how* they do it—establishing standards for transmitting signals.

The acronym stands for both the committee and the US standard video signal format it established.

OCR

This software allows text on hard copy to be read by a scanner and converted into a formatted computer file. Someday, **optical character recognition** might even work.

OEM

The hardware maker, or the **original equipment manufacturer**, is *not* the retailer. (OEM can, however, refer to a company that resells systems under its own brand name.) Often used in marketing analyses: *OEM sales versus retail sales.*

Sometimes a verb, as in Bill Gates's comment to then-Apple CEO John Sculley: "We also have experience in OEMing system software."

offline

An adjective meaning not connected to a network or computer. More metaphorically, it means out of touch: *I was offline for two weeks.*

As an adverb, it can also mean "in private" or "at a later time or different place": *Let's finish the hyphen debate offline.*

offscreen

A rough equivalent for **real life** (**RL**), the term can also refer to tasks a computer is handling behind the scenes.

one-to-many

An adjective referring to the publishing/broadcasting paradigm of mass media. The hegemony of one-to-many is now challenged by the **many-to-many** communications offered by the Web and other network technologies.

one-to-one

An adjective describing the communications paradigm of standard telephone service. One-to-one marketing is direct marketing in digital clothes.

online

Possessed of a computer and a modem. Jacked in.

The word is used today primarily as an adjective: *online community*. It also appears as a noun (synonymous with *cyberspace*) for the state of being defined by author Jon Carroll as "something between a seminar and a cocktail party—raucous and sensual and intense and defiantly, joyously human."

The solid spelling is becoming standard on copy desks and in company names: America Online, Ultima Online, Online TV.

onscreen

Literally, what's on a computer monitor. (For film and TV, *on the screen* or *on-screen* are still common.) Figuratively, any aspect of life that happens on a desktop, online, or in cyberspace.

OOC

Online shorthand for **out of character**, used especially in MUDs.

OOP

Spell out **object-oriented programming** but pronounce the acronym "oop." Think of it as the Lego theory of software—blocks of object-oriented code can be attached in different ways to build different programs. For example, an independent program like a spellchecker can be popped into a word-processing program or a mail program. Calendars, text, and sound may be embedded in the desktop.

Common standards include Apple's OpenDoc and Microsoft's COM (short for **component object model** and encompassing the older OLE technology).

open source

An adjective, sometimes shortened to **open** and sometimes abbreviated as **OSS** for **open source software**. It refers to nonproprietary computer systems—such as Linux or Apache—that are not limited to a single platform or controlled by a single manufacturer. Specifically, the term denotes software whose source code is freely available and can be modified. Easy to adapt and modify, open source software is also thought to be more stable and more secure than code developed behind closed doors by a single company.

The term was coined by Christine Peterson, of the Foresight Institute in Palo Alto, California, as a way to differentiate open source development from the free software movement it grew out of. Despised by patent-happy programmers and manufacturers, open source gained momentum with Netscape's 1998 decision to release its browser code.

See **"The Cathedral and the Bazaar," free software, GNU.**

operating system

The underlying software that gives a computer its look and feel and upon which all other applications and hardware depend. Although the technical definition of **OS** has become a legal issue, thanks to the Microsoft antitrust trial, think of the operating system as the conductor orchestrating the inner workings of the computer, the peripheral hardware, and you—the user.

Gene Amdahl created the first OS for the IBM 704 in 1954. Today, Unix, Windows, BeOS and other operating systems are more than just technical categories. They are cultures.

Or religions, as Umberto Eco mused in a column that appeared first in *L'Espresso* and then circulated on the Internet. In defining the "software schism," Eco called Mac Catholic, with its "sumptuous icons" and the promise of offering everybody the chance to reach the Kingdom of Heaven ("or at least the moment when your document is printed") by following a series of easy steps. DOS, on the other hand, is Protestant: "it allows free interpretation of scripture, demands difficult personal decisions . . . and takes for granted that not all can reach salvation." Following this logic, Windows becomes "an Anglican-style schism—big ceremonies in the cathedral, but with the possibility of going back secretly to DOS in order to modify just about anything you like."

ops

Internet Relay Chat jargon for **operator privileges**—such as the right to kick users off of a particular channel—that belong to the person who creates the channel. Can also refer to the operations arm of an IT department.

options

In the high tech world, options are not multiple choices, they are the currency of Silicon Valley—lucrative incentives to work 24/7 for years—or at least until the IPO. Specifically, the always-plural, often-elusive rewards translate into the right to buy X shares of company stock at a specified price. If the company goes public, those options can be converted to stock and provide an **exit strategy**. If it doesn't, employees are left with **vapor options**.

IPO or not, wrote "Andre La Plume" in *Wired*, options replaced penis size as the status symbols of the '90s.

OS

Think DOS. Remember OS/2. The acronym for **operating system** is as essential to tech talk as software is to computing.

When it comes to the plural acronym, the geeks disagree: OS's, OSes, or OSs? Avoid the debate by spelling it out.

OTOH

Shorthand of the online diplomat, it means **on the other hand.**

P3P

The **Platform for Privacy Preferences** standard proposed by the World Wide Web Consortium enjoys industry support that spans from Microsoft to the Center for Democracy and Technology. It allows netizens to set the rules for disclosure of their personal data. The P3P philosophy: *Some* information wants to be free.

packet

An envelope of data sent onto the Net. An email message is chopped into packets, each inscribed with the addresses of the source and the destination computer.

Vint Cerf compares packets to postcards, which also have "to" and "from" areas and a finite length. But there's one serious difference: Packets "go a hundred million times faster."

packet-switching

The circuit-switching killer. An asynchronous network architecture in which data is broken down into tiny, individually addressed pieces or packets of bits, which are sent separately across the network and reassembled on arrival.

The architects of packet-switching and the Arpanet persevered in the early '60s despite claims by AT&T and IBM that packet-switching would never work. One of them, Len Kleinrock, composed this ode to the packet:

> It was back in '67 that the clan agreed to meet.
> The gangsters and the planners were a team damned hard to beat.
> The goal we set was honest and the need was clear to all.
> Connect those big old mainframes and the minis, lest they fall.
>
> BBN had promised that the IMP was running late.
> We welcomed any slippage in the deadly-scheduled date.
> But one day after Labor Day it was plopped down at our gate.
> Those dirty rotten scoundrels sent the damned thing out air freight.
>
> We cautiously connected and the bits began to flow.
> The pieces really functioned, just why I still don't know.
> Messages were moving pretty well by Wednesday morn.
> All the rest is history: packet-switching had been born.

pageview

A standard measurement of Web traffic. A Web page might contain a headline, some body text, an ad banner, and a Java applet—elements that a client computer must request and download individually. Each request is one hit; the combination of hits and downloads that make up a screen is one pageview.

Of course, spelling it right doesn't guarantee that the user actually read the viewed page.

Palm

After the bust that was Apple's Newton, Palm Computing resuscitated the handheld market with the Palm Pilot in 1996. The company joined the 3Com family in 1997, and rechristened the bestseller after being sued by Pilot Pens in 1998. The 3Com Palm devices—all powered by the PalmOS—include the Palm III, Palm V, and Palm VII.

3Com, though, doesn't have a monopoly on the word:

Microsoft now sells the Palm-sized PC, and **palm computing** has been seized upon as a name for the smaller-than-a-laptop market.

palmtop

Originally an adjective, but now more often a noun for a gizmo that fits in one hand and is slightly smaller than a **handheld**.

paper money

Stock. Not cold hard cash. What companies with no earnings use to lure hopeful executives. How Infoseek bought WebChat Broadcasting System and how Lycos adopted *Wired* magazine's sibling, Wired Digital.

paradigm

Pompous and overused term for "model," as in *The Web represents a new paradigm in retailing* or *The digital revolution has forced a paradigm shift.* Sound a little fuzzy? So is the word.

patch

A programmer's Band-Aid solution. The quick fix for a bug. Also a verb.

PC

Forget "political correctness." PC has its own meaning in the tech world, though that meaning has shifted over time. It once meant "not IBM." Then it meant "not Macintosh." Now it really *does* mean any **personal computer**.

Ted Nelson wrote the first book about personal computers—*Computer Life*—in 1974. Less than 2 years later, two Steves in a garage launched the PC revolution with the Apple II. Four years later, Big Blue introduced the IBM PC. But just as minicomputers gave way to PCs, the glory of PCs will fade as the "information appliance" market matures—or so say the pundits.

PC card

Née **PCMCIA** (and still called that by many), this credit-card-size network adapter card slides into the PC-card slot of a portable computer and expands memory, adds video capabilities, works as a modem—and more.

Although PC cards and **expansion cards** add similar functions, expansion cards are used with desktop machines and must be attached to the motherboard.

PCS

A digital wireless mobile phone system. Short for **personal communication service**, this catchall term includes CDMA, TDMA, and D-AMPS networks operating on the 1900 MHz band of radio spectrum. This distinguishes PCS from cellular systems, which operate in the 800 MHz band.

Note: **PCS service** is redundant.

PDA

Avoid spelling out **personal digital assistant**. And avoid the acronym, too, which was coined by former Apple president and CEO John Sculley but invites confusion with the preppy's "public display of affection." Try **handheld** computer or **palmtop**. Wanna get more precise? Go for the brand name: the Philips Nino, the Palm VII, or the Handspring Visor.

Perl

This powerful scripting language was developed by Larry Wall and originally distributed over Usenet. Pronounced "pearl," the **Practical Extraction and Report Language** quickly became a hacking gem. On the Web, it's used to write everything from quick-and dirty cgi-bin scripts to bots to publishing systems.

PGP

Created by Phil Zimmermann and released on the Net in 1991, **Pretty Good Privacy** has been called "high-level encryption for the masses." The difference between sending a plain-old file and sending a PGP-encrypted document is the difference between sending a postcard and sending a letter in a cross-hatch security envelope.

phone numbers

Treat phone numbers consistently, simply, and completely. Every phone number should begin with a plus sign (a stand-in for the number you dial locally to get international access; like 011 in the US) and the country code. For Brazil, say, begin with +55. The next set of numbers, enclosed in parentheses, is the area, province, or city code: in São Paulo, this would be (11). Finally, for the local number itself, the digits should be organized according to the convention of that country, with spaces in lieu of punctuation: for the São Paulo chamber of commerce, 246 9199. So the entire number would be +55 (11) 246 9199. The number for the chamber of commerce in Saint Paul, Minnesota, is +1 (651) 223 5000. A few pointers:

- The country code for the US is +1.
- Since countries differ on how they punctuate phone numbers (some use hyphens, some commas, some periods), a single space between groups of digits is preferable to a punctuation symbol.
- Area, province, and city codes may vary from single digits (as in Paris) to quadruple digits (as in London), and are often preceded with a zero when dialed domestically.
- The initial zero should be dropped in listings intended for an international audience. The Florence chamber of commerce can be reached by dialing (055) 27951 inside Italy, but the proper listing for an international audience would be +39 (55) 27951.
- City-states like Singapore lack city codes altogether: +65 337 8381.
- 800 numbers in the US are accessible only from inside the country; they should not be preceded by the country code, since that would suggest they could be dialed from anywhere. For example, Wired 's 800 number should be listed this way: (800) 769 4733.

phreak

Someone obsessed with hacking the phone system. Also known as **phonephreak** or **phreaker.**

As *New York Times* tech reporter John Markoff writes, "The

original phone phreaks thought of themselves as 'telecommunications hobbyists' who explored the nooks and crannies of the nation's telephone network—not for profit, but for intellectual challenge."

PICS

The **Platform for Internet Content Selection** system allows Web sites or third parties to label (read: rate) site content and helps Web surfers filter sites. Consider it a prissy Good Housekeeping seal of the World Wide Web Consortium.

To Tim Berners-Lee, W3C figurehead and father of the Web, PICS establishes "a set of standards for describing data" and would stem anti-Internet legislation by putting the onus of censorship in the hands of individuals and parents. But netizens cried foul, arguing that while PICS could be used to filter porn or hate speech, it could just as easily be used by repressive governments to filter (read: repress) information.

It's a paradox of the Web that what was created as an antidote to the onerous **CDA** is potentially the most effective censorship technology ever designed. In the end, few sites picked PICS.

ping

A message sent by one computer to another computer to see if it is active. Also used colloquially: you ping a friend to see if he's around or, in a secondary meaning, to remind him of a meeting. The name was borrowed from sonar terminology.

pixel

The shortened form of *picture element*, for the dots that make up an image or character on a computer or TV screen. The more pixels, the better the resolution.

plaintext

Simple, unformatted, unword-processed, unencoded text. In contrast, **rich text** includes special fonts and styles.

planned obsolescence

An "in with the new, out with the old" marketing strategy. An industry tactic to drive sales by designing products that are incompatible with older systems. Think of gaming platforms, which are never compatible with the game cartridges you bought for the older console.

Although the computer industry—with its six-month product generations—has pushed the practice to new highs (or lows?), planned obsolescence has been the foundation of industrial development since Alfred Sloane ran General Motors.

platform

An almost indefinable noun, equal to the sum of the operating system, hardware architecture, and software running on a machine. The US is basically a three-platform market, dominated by Windows, Mac, and Unix. A few others control slivers of the market. **Cross-platform** software or hardware will run on multiple systems.

plug-in

An application that works seamlessly with a Web browser. Flash, for example, enables a browser to run small animations.

Pong

The triceratops of computer games. This simulated Ping-Pong, created by Al Alcorn and Nolan Bushnell in 1972 (*before* they founded Atari), established arcade games as more than a fad and laid the groundwork for a new entertainment phenomenon.

The *Pong* generation of two-dimensional games such as *Space Invaders* and *Asteroids* ended in the 1980s, with the introduction of processors that supported more complex games such as Sega's *Turbo*.

POP

Pronounced "pop" and standing for **point of presence**, this is playful jargon for local access to a network or telecom service. The more POPs an ISP offers, the more customers will be able to access the service through a local call. In 1999, AT&T WorldNet offered 691 POPs in the US. MCI Worldcom operates more than 1,000 worldwide. A gigaPOP boasts—duh!—gigabit capacity.

In a second, unrelated context, POP refers to a type of email account based on the POP protocol.

pop-up

Adjective describing a menu or dialog box that appears on the computer screen during certain procedures. Hit Print, for instance, and a pop-up window appears on the screen, from which you select the paper size or the number of copies you want.

port

As a noun, the spot where information passes in and out of a computer: *printer port, modem port, universal serial bus port.* (The latter, often appearing as **USB**, is replacing **SCSI** as the port of choice for peripherals.)

As a verb, **to port** is to translate a program from one platform machine to another. Colloquially, the word can also refer to the software that has been ported: *The Linux port of Office2000 is a total myth.*

portal

The welcome mats of the Web. These vast sites lead the way to the Net for millions who use the proprietary interface, channels, and search technologies to find news, entertainment, or other information. The largest portals include Yahoo!, Excite, Lycos, AOL, and MSN.

In 1998, Wall Street decided that portals were gold mines, and suddenly every company wanted to be one or buy one. It remains to be seen whether the term will outlast the business-model fad or go the way of *cyberstation*, *megasite*, and *gateway*.

Sloppy usage note: *portal* and *search engine* are not synonyms. Yahoo! and other yokels do offer search technologies to help you find content on their sites and beyond, but see **search engine** for the lowdown on those indexing-and-retrieval systems.

post

As a verb, **post** refers to the act of sending a missive to an online forum. Posting a single article to several newsgroups—a cardinal sin on Usenet—is known as **crossposting**.

Prepositionally speaking, a Webmaster or editor would publish an article *on* a site, while a reader might post a response *to* a site or newsgroup or *in* a chat room. As a noun, the **post** or **posting** is the message itself.

PostScript

The language of desktop publishing, created by John Warnock, the founder of Adobe Systems. PostScript allows computers and printers to treat documents as independent objects (fonts and numerous images) rather than as one single entity. Want an analogy? Think of movable type and a carved wood block.

POTS

Geekspeak for **plain old telephone service**. Pronounced "pots."

PPP

Don't spell out **point-to-point protocol**. That would be like spelling out UPS. The standard protocol for transmitting data over the Internet using phone lines and a high-speed modem, PPP replaced the similar, but slower, SLIP technology, with which it is still sometimes linked (SLIP/PPP).

prefixes

Close up prefixes with their stems whenever possible, unless the result is ungainly or confusing. The prefix *anti-* is generally joined to the stem word in examples like *antidigital* and *antivirus*, but imagine the vowel-heavy mess if we lost the hyphen in *anti-aliasing*. Likewise, the prefix *meta-* looks fine linked to words such as *metalinguistics*, but *metatheme* looks more like a cold remedy than what it is: a *meta-theme*.

The high tech world is awash with prefixes involving size and number:

atto—one quintillionth
exa—one quintillion
femto—one quadrillionth
giga—one billion
mega—one million
micro—one millionth
nano—one billionth
peta—one quadrillion
pico—one trillionth
tera—one trillion
yocto—one septillionth
yotta—one septillion
zepto—one sextillionth
zetta—one sextillion

privacy seal

The Boy Scout's honor of e-commerce, if such a thing exists. Bodies such as Truste, BBB Online, and CPA Webtrust issue a stamp of approval to sites that meet their criteria of consumer privacy protection. Relevant points might include publishing a clear privacy policy, disclosing what personal information is collected and how it is used, and overall site security.

programming

Coding, writing software, and sometimes hacking.

Writer and programmer Ellen Ullman describes the work as "maddeningly undefinable, some mix of mathematics, sculpting, scrupulous accounting, and wily ingenious plumbing."

programming languages

Humans speak to computers in programming languages. (Computers talk to each other in protocols. See below.) Unless the name of a language is a short acronym, initial caps are preferred: Ada, Basic, C, C++, Cobol, Fortran, Java, Lisp, Perl, Visual Basic.

protocol

Protocols such as HTTP, IP, PPP, and TCP—defined rules or standards of conversation—are what computers use to communicate with other computers, printers, and modems.

The Jargon File, that lexicon of geekspeak, defines **to do protocol** as "to perform an interaction with somebody or something that follows a clearly defined procedure." To restaurant diners, *Let's do protocol with the check* means "Let's ask for the check, calculate the tip and everybody's share, collect money from everybody, generate change as necessary, and pay the bill."

public key cryptography

The 1976 brainchild of Whitfield Diffie and Martin Hellman, public key cryptography is a thorn in the side of the NSA. A complex mathematical method to encrypt or secure digital communications, it differs from single key schemes like **DES**, in that it uses two algorithmic keys: a public one to encode the data and a private one to decode it. No hyphen, because the method is often referred to simply as **public key**. See **DES**, **encryption**, **key escrow**.

pulldown

An adjective describing an interface device or **menu** you can pull down using a mouse or a keystroke.

push

As its name suggests, this technology "pushes" media to you—or to your desktop or pager. This contrasts to **pull** media, which is what you find when you browse the Web. The push-ers rave about media that skips across TV channels, desktop screens, car windows, and watches to reach consumers. Nonbelievers call it media that interrupts and subverts the many-to-many promise of the Internet with its one-to-many, old-media model. In any case, it's a technology du jour that quickly became the technology du hier.

Trademarked versions of the technology include Pointcast and Microsoft's Active Desktop.

QOS

An abbreviation for **quality of service**, QOS is a sort of guarantee of smooth telecom life. The seemingly benign concept, though, has split the engineering community. One camp staunchly defends the AT&T tradition of hard guarantees about the quality of service customers can expect. The other believes that cheap, unlimited bandwidth will make QOS guarantees obsolete—there will always be enough bandwidth for a network connection.

No matter where you stand on QOS, spell it out.

queue

The designated area in which data enters a computer, is sequenced, and is dispatched. Queue derives from the Latin *cauda* (tail) and from the French *queue* (tail or waiting line). It is not spelled *Q*.

QWERTY

The standard keyboard—pronounced "kwer-tee"—and named after the first six letters in the upper row. Designed in 1872, the

QWERTY configuration of letters was designed to make typists slow down so as not to jam the keys of the newfangled typing machine. A simplified layout designed by August Dvorak and William Dealey in 1936 rearranged letters in order of frequency of use but wasn't widely adopted.

Some style it Qwerty, but we like the visual effect of that line of capital letters.

RAM

Your computer's short-term memory and the simplest route to faster processing. (It takes about 10,000 times longer to read from the hard drive than from RAM chips stored on the CPU.) Don't spell out **random access memory**, and keep the caps—even though RAM is pronounced like the male sheep.

The most common form of RAM, **DRAM** (dynamic RAM) provides the very short-term memory that lets you run more programs simultaneously. The more expensive **SRAM** (static RAM) does not need to be refreshed as often as DRAM. **VRAM** (video RAM) superpowers those multimedia apps. **NRAM** (network RAM) breaks up large applications and stores them in the RAM of many PCs on a network.

Computer memory is a singular concept and never takes a plural *s*. Go ahead—write about the price of DRAM chips or the price of DRAM, but not the price of DRAMs.

And remember this: memory (RAM) is not a synonym for "storage" (a hard disk or floppy).

RBOC

Pronounced "R-bock" and sometimes replaced with **RBHC** (regional Bell holding company) or **Baby Bell**, the **regional Bell operating company** is the spawn of the breakup of AT&T in 1984. The RBOCs do not include the long-distance providers AT&T and MCI Worldcom. They do include miles of wires that link the online world—down to the **last mile**. Many are beginning to offer Internet access, cable TV, and long-distance services themselves. See **Baby Bells**.

readme

A file containing vital information about a software program or file. Some companies plaintively prefer **README**, others **Readme**, and others **Read Me**!

real time

No lag time. No processing time. The minute-by-minute amount of time it takes you to open *Merriam Webster's Collegiate Dictionary* and read the following definition: "the actual time during which something takes place." Hyphenated as an adjective: *real-time conferencing*.

resolution

Image or audio quality; the more data used to create a picture (or audio track), the higher the resolution. Related slang includes **hi-res** (rhyming with "my Pez"), an adjective commonly paired with "file" or "image," and its opposite, **lo-res**. Image resolution is measured in **dpi**; audio quality is measured in **kbps**—the rate at which the audio is being read.

RGB

Red, green, blue. Think computer screen. Sometimes used as a synonym for "color," as in **RGB monitor**. Technically, the RGB signal is delivered by three distinct wires—one red, one green, one blue—and each pixel is colored by some mix of the three.

RISC

See **CISC** versus **RISC**.

RL

Online shorthand for **real life**.

robot

A mechanical being or device. The word was coined by Czech playwright Karel Čapek in his 1920 drama *R.U.R.* (Rossum's Universal Robots). The field of robotics has grown out of Čapek's fanciful idea.

robotics

A field of artificial intelligence devoted to the study of automated systems and machines.

The term was coined by SF writer Isaac Asimov in his 1942 story "Runaround." In *I, Robot,* a later collection of stories, Asimov presented the three laws of robotics:

1) A robot may not injure a human being, or, through inaction, allow a human being to come to harm.
2) A robot must obey the orders given it by human beings except where such orders would conflict with the First Law.
3) A robot must protect its own existence as long as such protection does not conflict with the First or Second Law.

ROM

Don't spell out **read-only memory**; do pronounce it "rahm." A storage device whose contents cannot be altered, ROM most often refers to the chips that hold a computer's built-in instructions. These chips are used in everyday appliances like cars, gas pumps, and microwave ovens.

The ROM family includes: **PROM** (programmable ROM), **EPROM** (erasable programmable ROM), and **EEPROM** (electrically erasable programmable ROM), which differ from standard ROM chips in that they can be written to only with special devices, can be rewritten a limited number of times, and retain their memory even when the power is off. **Flash memory**, a form of EEPROM, can be programmed and erased in large blocks, rather than byte by byte.

Faux-amis factoid: A **CD-ROM** contains no ROM chips of any kind.

ROTFL

Online shorthand for **rolling on the floor laughing**; more energetic than **ROTF** (rolling on the floor).

router

The traffic cop of networking, a router is a machine that knows hundreds of thousands of possible pathways from Point A to

Point B and is responsible for directing packets of data across the Internet. The newest **switch routers** include the once-distinct switching hardware that actually moves packets along their assigned routes.

Bolt, Beranek and Newman built the first router (rhymes with "doubter") in 1969; it looked like a refrigerator and bore the name IMP, for **interface message processor.**

RPG

Think of Dungeons & Dragons—an early multiplayer, character-based game. These days, **role-playing games** like Ultima Online are played over the Net.

RSI

The occupational hazard of computer users, musicians, and carpenters. Although **carpal tunnel syndrome**, a wrist affliction, is the most common form of **repetitive strain injury**, the back, neck, and eyes can also suffer from various ailments.

Also known as **repetitive stress injury** or **repetitive strain illness**.

Rte. 128

On the outskirts of Boston, the main line for minicomputer companies. In 1957, Kenneth Olsen (an ex-IBMer) and Harlen Anderson founded the Digital Equipment Corporation in an old mill building in Maynard, Massachusetts. Digital's PDP-8 heralded the end of the Iron Age of mainframes and helped make Rte. 128 an early Silicon Valley of the East.

RTFM

Online shorthand for **read the fucking manual**. More common, if less tame, than **RTM** (read the manual).

S!MT!!OE!!!

Online shorthand for **sets! my teeth!! on edge!!!** The punctuation is critical in expressing the sentiment of the person sending an email or typing a post, who would have used **SMTOE** if feeling a little more in control.

sci-fi

The adjective used by people who aren't into **science fiction**. See **SF** to avoid the faux pas.

screensaver

Eye candy. One of those cutesy visual displays—dancing babies, flying toasters—that once prevented monitor burn-in and now just harness idle computer cycles.

screenshot

An image captured from or displayed on a computer screen. Also known as a **screengrab**.

scribble

The saving grace of flame-throwers on The Well, the **scribble command** lets posters delete their words after the fact. The original post is replaced by a <scribbled> notice. Scribbling lets you eat your words, but not without leaving behind some digital crumbs.

scripting language

A code-and-run program that does not need to be compiled (i.e., translated) from source code into machine code. Scripting languages are less efficient than compiled programs like C, but their human-readable format gives nontechnical users a less daunting way to work with computers and enables trained programmers to create simple applications more quickly (and reduce their caffeine intake). Styles vary: **JavaScript, Lingo, Perl, Tcl.**

SCSI

Pronounced "scuzzy," the acronym refers to the **small computer system interface** that allows peripherals to communicate with a computer's operating system. The interface—if employed in a so-called **SCSI chain**—lets the CD-ROM drive connect to the computer connect to the external disk drive connect to the scanner.

Increasingly, however, peripherals are riding on the universal serial bus or **USB** standard. And in LAN circles, the faster

Fibre Channel is replacing SCSI as the interface standard of choice.

search engines

An attempt to make order out of chaos, these engines help Net surfers target information by keyword or concept. Unlike databases such as Lexis-Nexis and Dialog, search engines are free—as long as you have Web access. However irregular, they should be styled according to the company's preferences: AskJeeves, AltaVista, Go.com, HotBot, Inktomi.

server

A computer or workstation that "serves" stored data and files or processing power to other machines—or "clients"—on a network. Could be a Web server, a mail server, or a file server. The machine-filled back rooms of Internet service companies are known as **server farms**. Also refers to the software running the server. See **client/server**.

set-top box

The hardware that transforms your TV into a computer. The Pandora's box of the video-on-demand, home-shopping, 500-channel, interactive-TV future.

SF

The shorthand for **science fiction** is used especially on the Net, with mailing lists like SF-Lovers.

SGI

Founded by Jim Clark (later of Netscape glory) and originally named Silicon Graphics, Inc., SGI is famous for the machines that give us the wow!-factor reptiles in Hollywood hits.

SGML

You needn't spell out **standard generalized markup language**, though it may be helpful to identify it somewhere as the superset of markup languages that contains HTML and XML (but not VRML—a modeling language). Developed by IBM, SGML became an international standard for document exchange in 1986.

Shockwave Rider

The 1975 proto-cyberpunk classic by John Brunner pits a Big Brother–like government and computer networks against a brave rebel programmer. Required reading for all network and application designers, it gave inspiration to a generation of hackers.

shrink-wrap

Literally, the plastic wrapping around a software product. Traditionally, shrink-wrapped stood in as a synonym for prepackaged software or other prêt-à-porter products. As more and more software is being sold over the Net, downloads are driving shrink-wraps into history, but the term has become a new-economy buzzonym: *It's a shrink-wrap e-commerce solution* means "It's an easy-to-use tool for online business."

As the writer Marcus Laffey illustrates in *The New Yorker*, even packaging can be the source of metaphor: "He had the shrink-wrapped look that crackheads get, as if his skin were two sizes too small."

.sig file

Pronounced "sigg file," this is one of those tags that appear at the bottom of an email or post—a netizen's letterhead. Made of ASCII characters, a .sig file can be made of pieces of prose or pieces of art. In print, reproduce .sig files in a fixed-width font like Courier or Monaco. A couple of examples:

```
sensual is running a feather down your lover s body.
kinky is using the whole chicken.
perverted is if the chicken is still alive . . .
twisted is using boneless skinless chicken breasts.
erika grumet

anathema@gwis2.circ.gwu.edu
http://homepage.interaccess.com/ peetah/anathema
anathema on irc
```

```
David P Beiter  .=-.    byter@mcimail.com    .-=.
Geochemist    _..-«(                          )'-.._
CAVE, Inc    ,/./««.]]]\\.         (\_/)        .//[[[.'-'\.\,
1/2 Fast Rd./.«i]«.].]]]]]\\:.     )..._(      .:/ /[[[[[.[.'[i'.\.
Ritner KY/««,]]«.]]].]]]]]]\'''''. «' «' .«««««««/[[[[[[.[[[.'[[,''\.
42639./',]]«. ]]]]].]]]]]]]]]]]]]( \=/ )[[[[[[[[[[[[[.[[[[[.[[[,'\.
     /«,i]]]«.i]]]]]].]]]]]]]]]]]]{ NSS }[[[[[[[[[[[[[.[[[[[[i.'[[[i,'\
   /« ]]]]]«.]]]]]]]].]]]]]]]]]]]]][ BCI ][[[[[[[[[[[[[.[[[[[[[[.'[[[[[.'\
 ,/«,]]]]]«i]]]]]]]]]].]/«      '\]]:': ! :«:[[/«     '\[.[[[[[[[[[i'[[[[[,'\,
1:/«    '\:/«      '\:/«           \]]:@ :[[/          \:/«       \:/    \:1
1/        V          v           }=«\ :I :/'={           v          V     \1
```

Siggraph

An annual computer-graphics extravaganza, sponsored by the Association of Computing Machinery, and a mecca for digital art and interactive technology.

Pronounced "sigg-raff," the name derives from the Special Interest Group on Computer Graphics.

signal-to-noise

A ratio of valuable information to useless information, stuff to fluff: *The signal-to-noise ratio is plummeting.*

silicon

Nerd's gold. A common element (Si) with an uncommon ability to conduct electricity. Silicon, used in the majority of semiconductors, has become a metaphor for the cutting edge.

Silicon Valley

The high tech Garden of Eden, aka "the Valley." An urban sprawl spilling over five counties and four area codes, it borders San Francisco and embraces San Jose. Given over to PCs, silicon chips, skunkworks, supercampuses, and the get-rich-quick ethos of the big gamble, the Valley far outreaches its nondescript physical location—it is a state of mind that encompasses Microsoft, Amazon.com, Dell, and all of the other companies that have made bazillions out of silicon.

Coined by Don Hoeffler in 1972, the term has inspired New York's Silicon Alley, Chicago's Silicon City, Silicon Bog in Ireland, and a score more Silicon Somethings around the globe.

Sim-

The simulation prefix. Introduced in 1989, *SimCity* sparked the build-your-own universe game genre, including *SimLife*, *SimEarth*, *SimAnt*.

skunkworks

A secretive (or secret) R&D lab. A research center, far removed from corporate headquarters and market pressure, where teams of clever engineers experiment and innovate.

The first skunkworks was Skunk Works, Lockheed's research center in Palmdale, California, that produced, among other things, the F-117A Stealth Fighter.

slash

Also called a "solidus," "diagonal," or "shilling," this venerable punctuation mark is a fixture of life on the Web. It's the muse for Slashdot, the programmer's daily news site, and it even crops up in jokes:

> Q: What's the Internet address for the OJ page?
> A: http colon slash slash backslash escape.

SLIP

Outmoded by the newer, faster PPP, the dialup **serial line Internet protocol** allows access to the Internet over standard phone lines and a modem. Can also be an adjective: *SLIP connection*.

smartcard

A category of devices based on many technologies that includes phone cards, e-cash cards, and student IDs that serve as meal tickets, copier counters, and network-access cards. And they're getting smarter all the time.

We accept the prefix smart-, but worry about its overuse.

smileys

First created by Scott Fahlman on a Carnegie Mellon BBS around 1980, these small graphical renderings, composed of ASCII characters, substitute for facial expressions and gestures.

Tilt your head to the left to see a wink ;-) and a smile :-) and chagrin :-(.

Creative variations abound:

:-D [a person laughing)
>:D [a person laughing demonically)
:-D* [a person laughing so hard that he doesn't realize there's a six-legged spider on his lip)
%} [a person with eyes crossed and smirking)
>:P [a person sticking tongue out at someone)
<:/ & [a person with stomach in knots)
=:? # [a punk rocker—spiked hair, pierced lip, wearing a kilt)
(_!_) [an ass)
(!) [a tight ass)
(_x_) [a "kiss my ass")

SMTP

The language computers must speak to send and receive email on the Internet. **Simple mail transfer protocol** is used in conjunction with another protocol that downloads incoming messages or stores them on the server. That's why Eudora and other mail programs will ask for both SMTP and POP server addresses.

snailmail

Mail sent via the US Postal Service. William Safire calls it a "retronym," a noun phrase that is created to distinguish something (in this case, mail) from its more recent incarnation (in this case, email).

Sometimes used as a verb: *Gary faxed me the Asia itinerary and snailmailed the tickets.*

software

Digital DNA. Code. From the operating system to a word-processing program to a plug-in, the software encompasses the elements of a computer that you can't physically touch. (It can also refer to manuals and other code-related documentation.)

Note: software is a collective noun—never say "softwares."

Sonet

Short for **synchronous optical network**, this ANSI standard specifies the rate at which voice and data signals are transmitted over optical networks. It also detects and routes around line breaks.

source code

In the Web world, the HTML tags that are used to build a Web page. More generally, what computer programmers write using a programming language. The source code is then compiled into a machine-readable binary file of 1s and 0s.

spam

Electronic junk mail. Purportedly named in honor of SPAM, that tasteless luncheon-meat-in-a-can, and in homage to the *Monty Python* "Viking Spam" skit in which the word is repeated incessantly, interrupting other conversations and driving folks crazy. The term first appeared on Usenet, where newbies would post long and off-topic messages to many newsgroups, making intelligent discussion difficult.

Spam has entered the vernacular with a vengeance, though the term is often used incorrectly. Technically, spam involves sending one message to multiple recipients. It does *not* involve sending multiple emails to a single user or server in an attempt to shut the server down; that is a **mailbomb**.

spec

As a verb, to analyze the facts of a project before diving in. The plural noun, **specs** refers to the facts themselves.

spellchecker

The computer application that checks the spelling in a document. The related verb, **spellcheck**, means to run that not-as-smart-as-a-copy-editor function of the word-processing application. Sometimes **spelling checker**.

spider

Search engine technology. A simple program that scans the Web, crawling from link to link in search of new sites and recording the URLs.

Inktomi, a Web technology developed at UC Berkeley, owes its name to a mythological spider of the Plains Indians.

splash

The screen door you pass through to reach the front door of a Web site. A splash page may contain technical info (*Best viewed with Netscape Navigator 4.5* or *Click here to avoid the bandwidth-hogging Java applets*) or may contain spiffy visual effects (bandwidth-hogging Java applets).

spread spectrum

A wireless telecommunications technique that spreads signals across the spectrum. Conventional wireless, by contrast, is monogamous—sticking to a single band of spectrum. By hopping from frequency to frequency, messages sent using spread-spectrum technology are less susceptible to interference and more difficult to intercept. See **CDMA.**

stand-alone

A computer that is not linked to other computers or a network. The most secure place to store sensitive information.

Star Trek

One of the first TV science fiction series, *Star Trek* inspired a cult following and several films and spin-offs. *Star Trek: The Next Generation* often appears as *ST:TNG* or just *TNG*. Fans of *Star Trek*, previously known as Trekkies, now prefer the moniker Trekkers.

Jeff Greenwald on *Star Trek*: "So deeply ingrained is the *Starship Enterprise* in contemporary American culture that the first space shuttle was named after it. Its elegant design is to this generation what the Corsair was to the children of World War II."

startup

A handful of baby-faced, baggy-eyed entrepreneurs looking for seed funding. A company born in a garage, according to Silicon Valley lore. A noun so common we close it up.

sticky

Think of caramel and kids—a sticky Web site attracts readers and keeps them. **Stickiness** is a measurement of how long a person lingers on a site.

stream

Or **datastream**. The live flow of digital information.

streaming media

Web technologies that let viewers hear and see audio and video data as it arrives, rather than waiting for an entire file to download. RealAudio and RealVideo deliver such streaming data.

stylus

The oversize plastic toothpick used to input and access information from a touchscreen. The plural, according to the makers of the Palm, is **styli**.

suit

Not a techie. Someone in management or bizdev (business development) or marcom (marketing/communications). Someone who thinks in profits rather than programs and cares more about the bottom line than lines of code.

Sun

Sun—not SUN—Microsystems, Inc. was founded in 1981 by three Stanford grad students and a UC Berkeley software whiz. Although the inspiration for the current name was "Stanford University Network," the founders decided to abandon the acronym. (The company had already ditched its original name—Sun Workstations—because people thought it made office furniture.)

Sun opened the world of million-dollar mainframe computing to researchers and companies with only thousands to spend. Today the Fortune 500 company, based in Mountain View, California, is known primarily for its workstations, its Unix-based network servers, and its contribution to the Web world: **Java**, the simple object-oriented programming language. The company slogan: "The Network Is the Computer." The ad campaign: "We're the dot in .com."

supercomputer

These top-of-the-line teraflop machines—IBM's Blue Pacific, for example—compute at 3.9 trillion operations per second, some 15,000 times faster than your PC. Still used for advanced scientific research and other data-intensive engineering applications, supercomputers are going the way of mainframes, replaced by a do-it-yourself approach to supercomputing called **clustering**—linking together off-the-shelf PCs.

FWIW, Seymour Cray, who later founded Cray Computing (now a part of SGI), built the first supercomputer—the CDC 1604—for Control Data Corporation in 1958.

surf

A librarian named Jean Armour Polly was the first to use **surfing** to mean exploring the Internet. (As she explains at *www.well.com/user/polly/birth.html*, she got the idea from an old Apple memento that read "Information Surfer.")

But as William Gibson later noted, the experience of Web surfing may be more like "reading magazines with the pages stuck together" than like sliding along glassy, curling waves.

sync

The essential act of palmtop life: to ignite a conversation between a handheld device and a desktop or laptop computer. Although manufacturers disagree on the spelling (*Webster's* offers two), everyone agrees that if it doesn't sync, it's sunk.

sysadmin

The **systems administrator** (often shortened and pronounced "siss-admin") is the supergeek who keeps your office network—or any network—running smoothly.

sysop

System operator. Pronounced "siss-opp." The overseer, gatekeeper, referee, and Mr. Fix-It for a BBS. In the post-BBS world of national online services and Web communities, though, most sysops have become **sysadmins**.

system-on-a-chip

Buzzword for silicon circuitry that contains both processing power and memory, two traditionally separate functions.

T-1

A high-speed network link that theoretically transmits data at 1.5 Mbps. Originally a backbone technology, T-1s now carry data *and* voice for most medium-sized businesses.

The T-1 designation refers to the signaling speed rather than the medium of the network (copper, fiber). The European equivalent is an E-1, which transmits 2 Mbps of data. The faster T-3 transmits data at 45 Mbps. Then come OC-1, OC-3, OC-12, and other optical carrier-level standards.

TCI

The world's largest commercial cable company. After years spent slugging it out with the telcos, **Tele-Communications Inc.** sold itself to AT&T, forming a company with telecom, cable, and Net-service muscle.

TCP/IP

The mother tongue of the Internet: **transmission control protocol/Internet Protocol**. Announced by Vint Cerf and Bob Kahn in their May 1974 paper "A Protocol for Packet Network Communications," TCP/IP was made a mandatory standard by the National Science Foundation in 1985. Other Internet protocols, such as FTP or PPP, run on top of TCP/IP. See **Internet protocols**.

TDMA

A competitor to **CDMA**, the digital cellular technology called **time division multiple access** divides the spectrum into short sequential time slots and lets users transmit in round-robin fashion. Think of it as a cocktail party at which conversing couples take turns speaking—one sentence at a time. Like CDMA, TDMA is more philosophy than protocol—currently there are several flavors on the market.

Use the acronym—with a descriptive tag—rather than defaulting to the less-than-transparent full name.

techno-

Derived from *technology*, or *technological*. The technosavvy close up technowords: *technolust*, *technobabble*, *technocrat*. Leave hyphenated those that would create double vowels: *techno-anarchy*, *techno-averse*. As a noun for the music genre, *techno* stands alone.

TED

This annual four-day think tank usually held in Monterey, California, draws a clique of digital visionaries and a claque of wannabes. TED—which stands for **Technology, Entertainment & Design** and is pronounced like the nickname for Theodore—was created in 1984 by the architect and futurist Richard Saul Wurman. It has since grown immeasurably, and some digerati scoff that anyone with a few thousand bucks can buy in.

telco

Telephone company. AT&T, Bell Atlantic, Sprint—to name but three. The abbreviation is fine on first reference.

telecom

Short for telecommunications. Never plural (not *telecoms*).

telnet

Also known as **remote login**, telnet allows you to connect to another computer on the Internet to retrieve files or grab email.

TEOTWAWKI

The end of the world as we know it. The shorthand of Internet survivalists who believe Y2K spells doomsday.

Tetris

Some people argue that it was the perfect, infinitely playable computer game. Fascinated by the ancient Roman puzzle game Pentominos, Russian AI expert Alexey Pajitnov tweaked its simple geometric formations into real time using an archaic—-even-by-Russian-standards—Electronica 60 computer. With brackets delineating blocks, *Tetris* was born.

third-party

The adjective denotes hardware or software developed to work with another company's product. Those plug-ins, applications, and peripherals help turn an operating system into a platform. Third-party developers are the life of the party, producing the gadgets and goodies that'll make you buy Windows or Palm.

Third Wave

The postindustrial civilization or information age described in 1980 by futurists Heidi and Alvin Toffler. Their book *The Third Wave* details a First Wave agrarian civilization that was transformed by the cultural and economic institutions of the Second Wave: industrialization, mass production, mass media. Now that the assembly line is giving way to brainpower and high technology, we are entering the Third Wave.

When used adjectivally, none of these terms needs a hyphen: *Second Wave mentality*.

thread

An ongoing discussion on a Web site or in a newsgroup, in which posts are added one by one, in linear fashion.

3Com

The data-networking giant founded in June 1979 by Bob Metcalfe (the first computer-networking millionaire). His fortune—and 3Com's—was built on Ethernet cards, routers, switches, and the other nuts and bolts of networking.

What are the three Coms? Computer, Communications, and Compatibility.

throughput

The rate at which data is transferred or at which a processor can perform jobs. Close up, as with *output* and *input*.

time-sharing

A system design of yore, when computing power was centralized and expensive. John McCarthy proposed the first time-sharing system at MIT in early 1959, and at Stanford in 1961 built the first OS that allowed multiple people at different display terminals to jointly use a single computer. (Pre-McCarthy, "time-sharing" referred to splitting system processing-time between programs rather than people.

The first dialup time-share network—Tymshare—launched around 1968.

time zones

The convention for many US publications is to express time in stories by using Eastern Standard Time (EST) and Eastern Daylight Time (EDT). America Online, based in Vienna, Virginia, also uses EST and EDT when it lists scheduled live events. But this convention reflects the world of old media, based in New York and Washington, and ignores international audiences.

Pacific Standard Time and Pacific Daylight Time reflect the center of gravity of Silicon Valley, so that's what appears in *Wired's* pages.

On the Web, give times for online forums and events in the local time of the publisher as well as in Greenwich Mean Time (GMT). Here's a message that went out about an event on HotWired:

```
    Join us Monday, 12 February at 4 p.m. PST (Tues-
day, 00:00 GMT) in Club Wired's Feedback forum to chat
with the Cocteau Twins and listen via RealAudio to cuts
from their album, "Milk and Kisses."
```

TMOT

Online shorthand for **trust me on this.**

toolbar

Onscreen bar that displays various icons or formatting choices.

touchpad

The flat device that takes the place of a mouse on laptops.

touchscreen

The technology—used in everything from an information kiosk to your palmtop—that dispenses with the mouse and keyboard, allowing you to perform a function by touching the screen.

TPTB

Netizens averse to acronyms tend to retain the initial caps when spelling out **The Powers That Be**. Gives it that Big Brother energy.

trackball

Think of it as an upside-down mouse—a rotating ball that moves the cursor by spinning in its plastic base. Also a laptop feature.

TrackPoint

Aka **eraserhead**, this rubbery device—resembling the end of a pencil stuck mid-keyboard—was introduced by IBM with the ThinkPad laptop.

trapdoor

An entry point into a program, network, or system created by the system's designers or managers.

Trojan horse

The work of dark-side hackers. A seemingly innocuous program that hides a malicious virus, such as a password program that secretly records the passwords entered. Coined by the MIT-to-NSA hacker Dan Edwards, the word is proof that hackers read the classics.

TTYTT

Online shorthand for **to tell you the truth**.

Turing Test

In his 1950 paper "Computing Machinery and Intelligence," British mathematician and computer scientist Alan Turing proposed that if a computer could successfully impersonate a human during a free-form exchange of text messages, then for all practical purposes the computer should be considered intelligent. The Imitation Game, as he called it, soon became known as the Turing Test; it sparked endless academic debate and inspired an annual **artificial intelligence** competition of the same name.

Turing is invoked in various contexts, as in this passage from Douglas Coupland's *Microserfs:* "Michael's office lights were on, but once again, when we knocked, he wouldn't answer his door. We heard his keyboard chatter, so we figured he was still alive. The situation really begged a discussion of Turing logic—could we have discerned that the entity behind the door was indeed even human?"

24/7

The 9 to 5 of the '90s. Also the trademarked name of a Manhattan-based online advertising agency.

Style it with a slash—which fits the burnout workweek better than a hyphen or multiplication sign, the other options.

And think before you write 24/7/365. If the idea is "24 hours a day, 7 days a week" then the logical extension should be "52 weeks a year." If you *really* want the 365 then write 24/365, for "24 hours a day, 365 days a year."

Unabomber

Theodore J. Kaczynski, the antitechnology zealot who terrorized academics and high tech professionals for two decades, was arrested on April 3, 1996, at his 10-by-20-foot Montana cabin, and is serving four life sentences.

The name Unabomber derives from his original activity: mailing bombs to university professors and airline executives. The elusive terrorist was blamed for three deaths and the maiming of 23 people and took credit for a 35,000-word manifesto published in *The Washington Post* that led the FBI, indirectly, to him. His memoir, *Truth v. Lies,* expands on his belief that "the technophiles are taking us all on an utterly reckless ride into the unknown."

Note that Kaczynski is the Unabomber, but it was the Unabom case and Unabom victims.

unique users

The number of different people or computers to visit a Web site. A truer measure of readership than **pageviews**, the term unique users distinguishes between one person visiting a site five times, and five people visiting a site once.

Unix

The Swiss Army knife of the Net, this is a flexible, portable, and powerful operating system dominant around the world. Unix (pronounced "you-nix") was invented by Bell Labs programmers Ken Thompson and Dennis Ritchie in 1969, and released on November 3, 1971.

Some "trademark guardians" argued for UNIX, Dennis Ritchie explains, adding, "The word is not an acronym, and I prefer Unix. The lawyers wanted UNIX."

One witty programmer paid tribute to the power of this all-powerful OS in the story of "God as a Unix Weenie," which we've concatenated here:

```
In the beginning was the computer. And God said
LET THERE BE LIGHT!
You have not signed on yet.
GOD.
Enter password.
OMNISCIENT.
Password Incorrect. Try Again!
OMNIPOTENT.
Password Incorrect. Try Again!
TECHNOCRAT.
And God signed on 12:01 a.m., Monday, March 1.
```

God creates light and the firmament, and man and woman and the Garden of Eden, but in the end, it's Unix that controls creation:

```
CREATE GOOD NEVIL.
Done.
ACTIVATE EVIL.
And God saw he had created shame.
```

```
Warning! System error in sector E95. Man nWoman not
in Gard.En.
1 Error.
SCAN GARD.EN FOR MAN NWOMAN.
Man n Woman cannot be located. Try again!
SEARCH GARD.EN FOR MAN NWOMAN.
Search failed.
DELETE SHAME.
Shame cannot be deleted once evil has been activated.
DESTROY FREEWILL.
Freewill is an inaccessible file and cannot be de-
stroyed.
STOP!
Unrecognizable Command. Try again!
BREAK
BREAK
BREAK
***Attention all users. Attention all users. Computer
going down for regular day of maintenance and rest in
five minutes.
Please sign off.***
CREATE NEW WORLD.
You have exceeded your allotted file space. You must
destroy old files before new ones can be created.
DESTROY EARTH.
DESTROY EARTH. PLEASE CONFIRM.
Destroy Earth confirmed.
***Computer down. Computer down. Services will resume
on Monday, March 8, at 6:00 a.m. You must sign off
now.***
And God signed off at 11:59 p.m., Saturday, March 6.
And God had zero funds remaining.
```

uplink

To transmit a signal from a ground station to a satellite. Technically, information is then **downlinked**, though colloquially we'd say it is broadcast, to the home. Also a noun and an adjective.

upload

To transfer a file from a PC to a server, on a network or on the Net. As a noun, a synonym for those transmitted files.

URL

Do not spell out **uniform resource locator**, and do pronounce it "U-R-L" (not "earl"—unless you are repeating a punning nom de plume like Duke of URL). The URL is the address of a page on the Web, such as *www.wired.com* or an FTP site such as *ftp://ftp.mozilla.org.*

Note that the "U" in URL does *not* stand for *universal.*

Usenet

A globe-spanning collection of informal bulletin boards (or newsgroups) distributed over the Internet and devoted to almost every conceivable topic. Derived from "Users' Network," Usenet (pronounced "yooz-net") was launched by four Duke students in 1979. Tagged a "Poor Man's Arpanet" by some at the time, Usenet grew quickly, connecting a community of Unix programmers, and laying a path for the Internet around the world. More than 14,000 newsgroups exist today, accessible to anyone with a computer and a **newsreader**—the specialized Usenet browser that enables posting, thread-following, filtering, and kill files.

In keeping with the system's democratic flavor, newsgroups should be styled lowercase, with the dots in place: buddha.short.fat.guy, or rec.arts.erotica.

userid

A netizen's handle, used with a password, to access private servers or networks. Pronounced "yoozer ID" and sometimes shortened to **uid**.

users

Overused term for a "he," a "she," or a "they." Try to remember that users are people working at computers, not drug addicts. Also avoid **end user**.

uuencode

As Usenetters well know, this format translates binary files into ASCII, which can be easily posted or emailed without requiring special software.

V-

V- is for **virtual**. As in **VRML** (virtual reality modeling language) and V-chat (virtual chat). The exception: **V-chip** (see below).

V-chip

The **violence-censorship chip**. This save-the-children-from-sex-and-violence system is still more policy than product. By FCC mandate, all televisions shipped after January 1, 2000, must contain a microchip that can filter programming rated for violent or "objectionable" content.

VAX

The descendant of Digital's popular PDP-11, the VAX (**Virtual Address eXtension**) minicomputer dominated hackerdom from its release in 1978 until the arrival of microcomputers and workstations in the late 1980s. Digital still sells **Vaxen** or **Vaxes**, though it calls them "servers."

VC

Short for **venture capital** and code for funding: *Paul's startup just got some VC to build a vertical portal.* The acronym can also stand for **venture capitalist**, one of the fairy godmothers and godfathers of high tech. These private capital firms have helped launch many a high tech startup.

Kleiner Perkins Caufield & Byers, once *the* VC firm in the Valley, helped make Sand Hill Road a euphemism for success, but there are other players now: Benchmark Capital, Draper Fisher Jurvetson, Hummer Winblad. Not to mention other roads.

video-

Merriam Webster's defines the noun as "the visual portion of television," and we're seeing the combining form in more and more neologisms. But *video* is also an adjective, defined by good old *Merriam Webster's* as "being, relating to, or used in the transmission or reception of the television image." When is it a combining form and when is it an adjective? Here are our preferences: *video camera, video projector, video screen, video store, videocam, videocassette, videoclip, videoconference, videodisc, videogame, videophone, videostream, videotape, videotext.*

videogame

Part target practice, part odyssey, part animated cartoon. Everything from shoot-'em-up to sleuthing to fantasy role-playing. Played on game consoles like Sony's PlayStation 2 or on PCs. As for the solid spelling—one concept, one word.

viral marketing

A newfangled business-plan buzzword for what is essentially word of mouth. The term plays on the idea of the **meme** as an advertising tool. Think of companies such as eBay, whose "marketing" relies heavily on the gossip of obsessive collectors.

virtual reality

Term coined by Jaron Lanier to describe almost lifelike, immersive, simulated environments. Ivan Sutherland developed the first headmounted system in 1966. Also **VR**.

"Just what is Virtual Reality?" Jaron Lanier riffs. "I used to think I had the right to define the phrase, but I've since learned that language grows on its own terms. 'Virtual Reality' started out as a small company's trademark for an unusually provocative technology. It has since come to mean 'that which needs to be marketed.' It has also become a universal metaphor. A Hollywood tribute to Frank Sinatra exclaims that his singing 'creates a Virtual Reality'; the motivational guru Deepak Chopra is credited with giving readers a 'virtual reality toolkit for spirituality'; President Clinton is accused of being 'lost in VR.' The only other words in English that can be used as flexibly are obscenities."

Related terms include **augmented** or **mixed reality**, describing technology that superimposes computer graphics on real scenes rather than replacing reality with 3-D virtual mock-ups. This VR-made-practical has applications in surgery, architecture, and other serious professions.

virus

Digital infection. Code that is hidden within and spread by a host program. Can be harmless or destructive. The term was first used in reference to a hostile computer program in David Gerrold's 1972 novel *When Harley Was One*. But the term virus also emerged independently from the academic world of Fred "father of the computer virus" Cohen.

Note: the term is not synonymous with **worm** or **Trojan horse**.

VLSI

A category of tininess, **very large-scale integration** refers to microchips containing hundreds of thousands of transistors. **LSI** chips, by comparison, contain only thousands.

voicemail

Recordings collected by an electronic messaging system or answering service. Unlike messages left on an answering machine, voicemail can be forwarded to other message boxes or replied to.

VR

See **virtual reality**.

VRML

Use the acronym, pronouncing it "ver-mul." The 3-D complement to HTML. Mark Pesce read William Gibson's breathtaking description of cyberspace as a call to arms and spent subsequent years working with three colleagues to bring *Neuromancer's* consensual hallucination to life. The result is **virtual reality modeling language**, a protocol for creating navigable, hyperlinked 3-D spaces on the Web. VRML, however, is virtually dead.

W3C

If CERN is the birth mother of the Web, the **World Wide Web Consortium** is its devoted nanny. The industry organization is led by Tim Berners-Lee and his colleagues at the Laboratory for Computer Science at MIT in collaboration with CERN, INRIA (Institut National de Récherche en Informatique et en Automatique, the French National Institute for Research in Computing and Automation), Keio University, and other sponsors. Founded in September 1994, the W3C promotes standards, develops prototypes, and serves as an information resource for the Web.

WADR

Online shorthand for **with all due respect**. Not to be confused with **WRT**, meaning **with respect to.**

WAN

Don't spell out **wide-area network.** It is a network linking computers over a great physical distance—in contrast to a **LAN**, which is local, or a **MAN**, which covers a metropolitan area.

wares

Software catchall. William Safire claims that *-ware* entered the world in Sanskrit as *vasna*, meaning "price." According to John Barry in *Technobabble*, *ware* appeared in A.D. 1000 for articles of merchandise or manufacture, and *yren ware* (ironware) surfaced in 1398. From the 1500s onward, *hardware* meant merchandise or goods made of metal. When *software* entered the language around 1962, hardware took on the meaning of the electronic or mechanical parts of a computer, as opposed to the programs that ran on it. **Warez** refers to pirated software.

Wares include:

bloatware—software that hogs space on your hard drive.
firmware—software permanently stored in ROM.
freeware—software available free from the developer.
groupware—software that allows people to share documents and work collaboratively, like Lotus Notes.
shareware—freely available software that the developer asks payment for.
shovelware—the mediocre material people shovel onto a Web site or other medium after it's been somewhere else.
vaporware—software that never makes it off the drawing board.
wankware—X-rated software.
wetware—your brain.

watermark

A digital watermark marks an electronic document, often with a copyright notice, much as its analog twin marked paper.

wearable

The first wearable computer was the wristwatch created by Cartier in 1904. Or was it the pocket watch, invented in the 1700s? Or eyeglasses, first mentioned in 1268? Talking about wearables today, MIT professor Mike Hawley asks, "Will your cuff links really link? When you get a phone call, will your earrings ring? What more will you watch on your wristwatch? Will your Victoria's Secret someday kiss and tell?"

From mainframes to minicomputers to desktops to handhelds, computers have increased in processing power and decreased in size. Shrink-to-fit computers are just the next step.

Web

Aka the **World Wide Web**. Or **WWW**. This global online information repository—a vast, broad, not-always-deep, often useful, sometimes vexingly esoteric archive—is an application running on top of the Internet.

Tim Berners-Lee, a British programmer at CERN, conceived this first practical hypertext system in 1989, defining the protocol **HTTP**, creating the standard document-addressing format **URL**, and devising the programming language **HTML**. He released the software onto the Net in December 1990, though the Web did not take off until 1993, when the NCSA released **Mosaic**, the first GUI browser.

Web versus **web-**

Is it an attributive noun? Is it a combining form? Does it deserve a cap? Use *web-* as a combining form sparingly: for words that really have developed a currency (*webzine*), that are used over and over (*webmaster*), and that have a compelling benefit (*websters* differentiates the wizards from the dictionaries).

We prefer the proper noun for Web site, but go ahead and play with the style of these webwords (did we miss any?):

webcam—a video camera hooked up to the Web, such as the Jennycam.

webcast—a live broadcast on the Web, using audio- and video-streaming technologies.

webgod—"wizards" in Unix-speak, these are the programmers with seemingly supernatural powers.

webhead—a nicer way to say "addict."

webmail—email service or account, almost always free, through a Web site such as Yahoo! or Hotmail. Aka branded email.

webmaster—the creator of a site. And also its janitor. Derived from postmaster, the person responsible for handling the quirks and queries related to a Net domain.

webmonkey—a Net mechanic, less greasy than its automotive counterpart, and (with an initial cap) the trademarked name of the Wired Digital channel that tells you how to build Web sites.

webonomics—the laws governing the bit-based economy of the Web and defining relationships between consumers, producers, distributors, and advertisers.

webster—a denizen of the Web.

webzine—media of the Web and for the Web, sites such as Feed or **Salon**—that publish original content. Also e-zine.

Web ring

Predominantly homemade sites or pages focused on single or related topics and linked by their creators. Web Ring (*webring.com*), for example, serves as a launch pad to more than 60,000 rings, including more than one million pages. The phenom began in 1995, when Sage Weil wrote the first such code.

WebTV

Launched by Steve Perlman in '96 and sold to Bill Gates in '97, this television-on-the-Web company is a thorn in the side of wordsmiths writing about the blurring of the broadcast networks and the Net. Until the industry figures out what the hell a networked television is, call those generic attempts at convergence Web-based TV.

The Well

The Well

Founded in 1985 and sold to the webzine *Salon* in 1999, The Whole Earth 'Lectronic Link is celebrated as a model virtual community.

As Howard Rheingold wrote in *The Virtual Community*, "Finding The Well was like discovering a cozy little world that had been flourishing without me, hidden within the walls of my house; an entire cast of characters welcomed me to the troupe with great merriment as soon as I found the secret door."

whois

A command to find the Who behind the .com, .org, or .net. The whois program lets you access a database of registered domain names.

Windows

Microsoft DOS with a GUI, Windows is the family name for Microsoft's operating systems. Specific versions include Consumer Windows for 2000 (née Windows 95), Windows 2000 Professional (née Windows NT), and Windows CE. When it comes to nicknames, the standard PC systems are referred to as "Windows," while the business server software is shortened to "NT" and the handheld OS-lite to "WinCE" or just "CE."

Wintel

Any computer based on the duopoly of the industry: a Windows operating system and an Intel microprocessor. More than 90 percent of the personal computers in use today.

WIPO

Law and order for ideas. Created by the UN, the **World Intellectual Property Organization** is charged with developing global standards from a hodgepodge of national laws and updating copyright laws to the digital age.

wireless

Wired without wires. Communication—cellular or satellite—over the radio spectrum.

In 1969, Norm Abramson built the first wireless network—

Alohanet. Today, the wireless industry is a maze of competing standards and incompatible networks. The International Telecommunications Union is working on a global standard known as IMT 2000 (International Mobile Telecommunications 2000) that will support high-speed broadband access no matter where you're calling from. See **CDMA, cell phone, GSM, PCS, TDMA.**

wizard

In the Unix community, a technical guru or supergeek. In MUDs, the sysadmins and master players who combine writing code and writing fiction. In some software apps, a help function.

word processor

Software such as Microsoft Word or WordPerfect that allows you to create, edit, and format text files. In pre-PC times, a word processor referred to a specialized computer with wordsmithing functions.

workstation

Expensive, powerful desktop machine such as Sun's Ultra 60, SGI's Onyx2, and IBM's IntelliStation—think of the mini minicomputers used as networks servers and preferred for high-end graphics. Today, a PC with a powerful chip could qualify as a workstation.

World Wide Web

See **Web** for the basics on this graphics-intensive environment running on top of the Internet.

Robert Cailliau of CERN recalls how the name "World Wide Web" was chosen: "I'd set the rule that we would not use the name of yet another Greek deity or classical mythical figure. I searched for some acronyms and also looked into Germanic mythology, but the best I found there was Loki, a god whose role is not always positive. Then one evening, we decided to have a beer on the terrace of the cafeteria to finish the day. After another round at names, Tim suggested 'World Wide Web.' I thought it would be difficult to abbreviate, but Tim was keen on using it as a preliminary name. Then it stuck, and it was too late to change."

The WWW acronym—sometimes said to stand for "World Wide Wait"—is still visible in many URLs.

worm

Self-replicating, often destructive code that travels independently across a network. The first worm was written in the 1980s by two Xerox PARC researchers; they named their creation after the "tapeworm" program in John Brunner's 1975 novel *Shockwave Rider*.

In November 1988, Robert T. Morris's **Internet Worm** nearly brought down the Net. While the hacker claimed it was a benign experiment that spun out of control, Eric S. Raymond says it "did more to make non-hackers nervous about the Internet than anything before or since."

WORM

Caps help underscore that this acronym for **write once, read many** is not synonymous with the noun *worm*, for a squiggly little animal or a self-replicating piece of code.

WORM is an optical disk-storage technology. But if you use it, don't make mistakes—data can be recorded only once.

WTFIGO

Online shorthand for **what the fuck is going on?**

WYSIWYG

Pronounced "wizzywig," the acronym for **what you see is what you get** denotes computer display technologies that show documents onscreen as they will appear on paper.

Xanadu

Ted Nelson's hypermedia dream was named for the Coleridge poem ("In Xanadu did Kubla Khan/ A stately pleasure dome decree:/ Where Alph, the sacred river ran/ Through caverns measureless to man/ Down to a sunless sea"). As Nelson described in his 1982 book *Literary Machines 90.1*, Project Xanadu is "an initiative toward an instantaneous electronic literature; the most audacious and specific plan for knowledge, freedom, and a better world yet to come out of computerdom; the original (perhaps the ultimate) hypertext system."

Project Xanadu might also be described as the longest-running vaporware project in the history of computing. Although many believe Nelson's ambitions for Xanadu have been realized by the Web, he has described the Web as "pretty awful. The unfortunate thing is how messed up it is."

Xerox PARC

Founded in California, in 1970, **Xerox Palo Alto Research Center** helped develop GUIs, object-oriented programming languages, Ethernet LANs, and laser printers, in addition to specific technologies for Xerox copiers and printers. Oops! Did we forget the Alto? PBS journalist Robert Cringley worded it nicely when he said "Xerox PARC was Jerusalem, Rome, and Mecca all rolled into one."

Xerox PARC's motto: "The easiest way to predict the future is to invent it."

XML

A meta-data system language, similar to **HTML** but far more sophisticated. While an HTML tag can specify "this is a headline" or "this is an image," **extensible markup language** can specify "this is a headline about Microsoft and antitrust law that appeared in the June 1999 issue of *Wired*" and that "this is a picture of Bill Gates taken on 4/1/99."

The logic of XML is obvious, but so is the problem—all netizens must agree to use the same subject tags. For this reason, XML is unlikely to replace HTML as the vernacular of the Web, though the sophisticated language *is* used behind the scenes in applications and databases.

Y2K

The inability of some computers to register dates in 2000 and beyond, and the Monica-like, mega media story of 1999. Also known as **the millennium bug**. Technically speaking, however, it's not a bug but a design flaw—a problem caused by the coder rather than the code: In the 1950s, when the computer world was young and memory was expensive, programmers marked time with two digits for the day, two for the month, two for the year. Dropping the "19" saved two bytes of precious RAM. Everyone knew that in 2000, the two-digit year would roll over like the odometer on an old Chevy, and the computers would think they'd jumped 100 years into the past. Programmers warned their managers but were told not to worry.

YA

In the jaded shorthand of geeks, **yet another**. As in, *Microsoft released YA browser* upgrade.

Yahoo!

One of the Web's first homegrown brands, Yahoo! was founded by two Stanford grad students in 1994. The Mountain View, California, company is known for its directory listing of sites on the Web. It's also known as one of the few .com companies operating in the black.

Cofounder Jerry Yang has since been verbed. **To yang**, according to Guy Kawasaki in *Geek Speak,* is to build something out of nothing: *When I started this business, there were ten search engines, but I yanged ours into a multibillion-dollar valuation.*

YOYOW

The ur-online shorthand for **you own your own words**. First uttered (er, typed?) by Stewart Brand when he helped launch The Well in 1985, the credo became the touchstone of Well culture. Also sometimes **YOYW** (**you own your words**).

zine

A small, cheap, self-published work with a press run of 15 to 2,500; an underground, anarchistic version of a magazine.

The term derives from "fanzine," a word coined by Louis Russell Chauvenet in the early 1940s to describe the do-it-yourself publications made by science fiction fans. Today, the term has digital cousins: **webzine** and **e-zine**.

Style *FAQ*

Hands down, the question most frequently asked of the *Wired* copy desk is how we style *electronic mail.* Well, we shorten it to *email,* as explained in the Introduction, Principle 6 ("Anticipate the Future"). We also get many inquiries about hyphens, since new noun pairs seem to appear as fast as new peripherals.

These and other questions are collected here. Please keep those queries coming, by emailing us at *wiredstyle@wired.com.*

How do you print email addresses when they appear in prose?

In text, email addresses should be italicized, as should URLs. This imparts a sense of the whole address as a discrete unit. Some folks prefer angle brackets, which win over parentheses, because they make clear that adjacent punctuation is not part of the email address or URL: <wiredstyle@wired.com>.

When email addresses don't fit across one column and must be broken over two lines, never break them on a hyphen—this leaves unclear whether the hyphen is part of the address. Similarly, never break email addresses by adding end-of-line hyphens.

Also, don't break them after a dot, which will look like a period ending the sentence. Break email addresses just before the punctuation, pulling the dot or the @ sign down to the next line:

wiredstyle
@wired.com.

Why does *Wired* print email addresses in all lowercase letters?

For consistency's sake. And because it looks cleaner. We once received a trenchant argument from Thierry d'Allant, president of Planet Media, who disputed our style: "Although the Internet may not be case sensitive . . . the way you print an email name is of importance: mine is PlanetTdA because my initials are TdA and I work for Planet (Media); 'planettda' simply does not mean anything."

Sorry, Thierry. No *change d'avis* here: such individual preferences are more trouble than they're worth. After all, most of the Net (excepting the Web) is not case-sensitive—an email will travel to the right place regardless of the case of its constituent parts. *SteveCase* is no different from *stevecase* to an Internet email server. There are email addresses that make us question this approach (PObox.com does look better than pobox.com), but for now we're sticking with lowercase letters.

What are your guidelines for printing URLs, especially the long ones?

Uniform resource locators (*not* "universal resource locators") are the signposts of the World Wide Web, the directions you give your browser to navigate to a homepage or Web site.

- In text, the entire URL should be italicized. This gives it a kind of unity, which is important because so many are so long: "You'll find New Mexico's Monastery of Christ in the Desert on the Web at *www.christdesert.org/pax.html*."
- Like email addresses, FTP sites, and newsgroups, URLs do not contain internal spaces.
- Punctuation marks in URLs act as critical separators and should never be dropped. They include:

  ~ [the tilde, aka "squiggly" or "twiddle")
  - [the hyphen)
  _ [the underscore)
  . [the period or dot)
  / [the forward slash)
  \ [the backslash)
  | [the pipe)

- Domain names in URLs should be lowercase. Pathnames, (which follow the first slash) are case-sensitive, so follow the style dictated by the site.
- URLs end in a forward slash "/" if the last item is a directory, but not if it is an actual HTML file. But you don't really need to fret over this—your browser automatically adds the slash to the URL that appears in the location window.

Many URLs are hopelessly long and don't fit within narrow columns. How do you break them over two lines?

Break a line before or after the discrete units that begin URLs—http:// or ftp://—but do not force a break within these protocol tags. For Web sites, it is not necessary to include the http:// tag, since nearly all Web browsers will add it automatically. Dropping http:// also helps to shorten the URL. However, if the site requires another protocol (such as gopher:// or ftp://), use the appropriate tag.

Don't break a URL at a hyphen. This may introduce confusion about whether or not the hyphen is part of the URL.

Break URLs right before a punctuation mark, carrying the punctuation symbol to the next line. If this is impossible, break the URL with a soft return between joined syllables, as we had to do for this pull quote in an article on Thomas Paine:

> It's easy to imagine Paine as a citizen of
> the new culture, issuing fervent
> languages from his site, *www.common*
> *sense.com*. He would be a cyber hell-raiser, a Net fiend.

If a URL ends a sentence, always add the requisite period.

How do you treat domain names in text?

Domain names should not be equated with email addresses and URLs. They're more like generic nouns, so they demand a different approach. We style them roman.

In one *Wired* story, writer Joshua Quittner snatched up mcdonalds.com before the burger barons could even pronounce the dot. In an article recounting his shenanigans, here's how *Wired* treated the domain name and a specific email address at that site:

> What should I do with mcdonalds.com? You tell me. I could auction it off. I could hold on to it as a trophy, à la Curry and mtv.com. I could

set up a Mosaic homepage, explaining the difference between McDonald's and Josh "Ronald" Quittner.

Got a suggestion? Send it to *ronald@mcdonalds.com.*

For a more complete discussion about what all the parts of an Internet address mean, see **domain name**, page 72.

How do you document references—in a bibliography, say—to information from the Internet? Should a Web site be treated differently from an email or a listserv?

Wired Style is written primarily for journalists, so we haven't delved into the myriad questions facing authors writing in an academic context.

But here's some good news: *The Columbia Guide to Online Style,* by Janice R. Walker and Todd Taylor, answers all those Net-scholarly questions. The latest version of the *MLA Style Manual* also addresses such questions, and the precise part of the book you'll want to consult lives on the Web: *www.mla.org/set_stl.htm.* Two handy guides from St. Martin's Press will also set you straight: *Online! A Reference Guide to Using Internet Sources,* by Andrew Harnack and Eugene Kleppinger, and *The Everyday Writer: A Brief Reference,* by Andrea Lunsford and Robert Connors.

One short answer is that the guidelines for citations of electronic sources are evolving along with the technologies. For sources accessed through the Internet, the basic info you need for a footnote or bibliography includes: the author's name, the title of the work, the date of publication, the address (the URL or path followed to locate the site or file) or the type of source (CD-ROM, personal email), and the date of access, especially important since so much information online is fluid, changing continually and without warning.

Do email quotes differ from spoken quotes?

Email and online postings are a cross between print and conversation. They can be used much as spoken quotes would be used in an article, but because they are written, it is preferable to reproduce them verbatim—spelling warts and all.

If email quotes are straightforward and indistinguishable from spoken quotes, they can be freely mixed in among quotes from a f2f interview. In this case, it's fine to style the email quotes according to print conventions and—go ahead—correct the typos.

If, on the other hand, the email quotation or online posting evokes the electronic medium—the mood and mores of online communication—leave the idiosyncrasies, including:

› Odd spelling and syntax. Resist the urge to sanitize.
› The punctuation conventions of the font-free ASCII world:

asterisks	(used for emphasis, like italics in print)
/slashes/	(also used in place of italics)
underscores	(used for titles, or in place of underlining)
ALL CAPS	(used to indicate shouting)

Don't use [sic] when you're citing emails—you might end up with as many [sic]s as original words. And consider heightening the sense of email as its own messaging form by using a fixed-width font (we often use Courier, which resembles email) to set online quotes apart from the rest of the text.

If someone sends me an email—or posts something on the Net—can I cite it in a published article?

This raises some thorny issues and points to one of the biggest differences between online reporting and f2f reporting. The online world is characterized by the impression (or illusion) of privacy, and a reporter can easily take advantage of the environment to snooker sources. It is perfectly legal to quote sections of email disseminated publicly (except, of course, if the email is legally defamatory). But since it's not in anyone's interest to burn sources, we suggest these ethical guidelines:

› If you are a writer intending to use emails for publication, identify yourself as a writer and tell your source you wish to use the email—especially since your source can't see you with your notebook or tape recorder. At the very least, go back to the source later for permission to quote an email.
› Have any reposting or borrowing from threaded discussions

vetted by participants. (Many people believe that posting is tantamount to proclaiming publicly, and without a doubt the Internet is a master disseminator. But we try to give posters a say in whether or not their words are republished.)

- Don't assume that an online handle protects a source's anonymity. A handle is a pseudonym, and the person behind it may be completely identifiable in his or her Net community.
- Just as important, be very careful about using sources you know only by a pseudonymous handle, especially in controversial and potentially defamatory stories.

What's the deal with all the capital letters in the middle of words?

Call 'em what you want—intercaps, incaps, midcaps, BiCaps—these have become a fixture in the technology industry, in names like JavaScript, QuarkXPress, WordPerfect, and MCI WorldCom.

Use them with these caveats:

- Follow company and product style for intercaps (BeBox, CU-SeeMe, RealAudio) and mixed-case names (DirecTV, Inter-NIC), but not for names that are all caps and five letters or longer, such as Siggraph, which just looks too ugly as SIG-GRAPH.
- Print online names as they are used by their owners: tOxicHoney, GashGirl, ms_holliday.

And while we're on capitalization, give "the" an initial cap when it is part of a name: The Computer Museum, The Microsoft Network, *The New York Times*, The Well.

How do you style all those odd company names?

Most tech companies have Web sites; start there. They typically contain a copyright link at the bottom of the front door listing all company copyrights—exactly how they should appear in print. This would be an impeccable source if it weren't for human error; call the company to double-check. Ask someone in the public relations department to literally pick up something with the company logo and look at it—stationery, press releases, product packaging. Beg them not to trust their memories.

Occasionally, the PR person will insist you publish some bizarre combination of all capital letters (*USA TODAY* as all caps) or unusual characters (Alias | Wavefront). Don't listen—this is merely an attempt at making the company's name jump out of a column of uniform text. It's a judgment call: honor simple punctuation elements that are part of a company name—CorelDraw! or Canal+—but realize that you may lose readers with sentences like this one: "auto•de•sys's form•Z RenderZone modeling and rendering package might just renew your three-dimensional enthusiasm."

Well, does *Wired* ignore trademarks?

Hardly! We like the unpredictable way tech companies style their own names. At the same time, we acknowledge the lowercase leanings of the Net—and the tendency over time for words to move from the proprietary to the communal. Eons ago, usage caused *Chautauquas* to become *chautauquas*. More recently, *Kleenex* became *kleenex* and *Xerox* became *xerox*. Today, Palm is the trademarked name of the handheld devices created by Palm Computing and then bought by 3Com. But 3Com can't dictate style: *palm computing* describes the entire smaller-than-a-laptop market. When names—trademarked or not—are adopted as generic nouns in the vernacular, we pay attention.

Internet protocols offer an example of names that often start out as proper nouns but become so ubiquitous (especially when distributed as freeware) that people use them as generic nouns. Some proper nouns we accept as generic include **telnet**, **gopher**, and **listserv**.

Of course, not all Net tools are there yet. **Veronica** has gone from a bona fide acronym (Very Easy Rodent-Oriented Net-wide Index to Computerized Archives) to a noun that is initial capped to an irrelevant protocol. Same goes for Veronica's partner **Archie** (a protocol for searching FTP sites). Who would want to style these lowercase—losing in the process the tribute to '60s America's favorite teenage cartoon couple? Of course,

Archie and Veronica live on in archive servers (not to mention rerun cable stations).

Should you capitalize the first letter of a proper name like iMac when it begins a sentence?

"iMac, therefore I am." It's unconventional, but why not? We like the way many tech upstarts defy conventions for capitalization. For example, the pun implicit in id Software seems perfect: the creators of *Doom* really aren't ego or superego types. Why change it to Id Software? Just leave the first letter lowercase: *eWorld finally bit the dust.*

If you're uncomfortable with this approach, go ahead and recast the sentence. In an article about the diving-mag-that-took-a-dive, for example, we changed "*aquaCorps* took a different approach" to "Michael Menduno's *aquaCorps* took a different approach."

Resist caps for email addresses and newsgroups even when they appear in a headline. "The War Between alt.tasteless and rec.pets.cats" was one headline *Wired* ran; "alt.scientology.war" was another.

Did you ever meet an acronym you *didn't* like?

Like 'em or not, acronyms are an essential part of wired culture. While they do connote the scientific and the technical, their use is not limited to scientists and techies. Often, acronyms pick up steam simply with use and become words in themselves. Some are pronounced as a series of letters (CPU, DSL). Some are made up of initials but pronounced as words (ASCII, DOS). Some are the shorthand of the Net (FWIW, IMHO).

(For the record, we are somewhat crudely lumping together initialisms and acronyms. Technically, all clusters of letters are initialisms. Only those pronounced as words are acronyms. Copy editors of the world, forgive us.)

Acronyms pose a number of dilemmas. First of all, they can be incredibly obtuse. (Who knows what CDMA stands for? And if you do, try explaining what it means.) Also, acronyms can be incredibly imprecise. Sure, ATM stands for asynchronous transfer mode. But it might stand for automated teller machine. Or Adobe Type Manager. Finally, acronyms often lack the literary richness of words: WWW is colorless next to the Web, which actually suggests a labyrinthine medium.

Embrace acronyms, following these rules of thumb:

- Use acronyms common in the vernacular of your audience. In the techno realm, acronyms like RSI and LCD are as recognizable as the analog world's FBI and CIA.
- Find the elegant solution. It isn't necessary to write out "hypertext markup language" each time you invoke HTML, but you might, in an appositive phrase, tag HTML as "the Web's lingua franca."
- Listen for the colloquial, for those acronyms that enter the vernacular. Expressions like MOO possess all the character of the best words. IBM and IPO have earned not just denotation, but connotation. Besides, people *say* them.
- When an acronym has gone from being pronounced as a series of letters to being pronounced as a single word (Basic, Lexis, Nasdaq), use initial caps. Also, if an acronym is five letters or longer, we're inclined to initial cap it (Nynex, Siggraph). But we do make exceptions for those venerable—or merely creaking—artifacts of computing: ASCII, DOS, RAM, ROM.
- Resist the temptation—out of laziness or haste—to reduce any old long proper noun to an acronym. Don't buy the bureaucratese hook, line, and sound byte. Use a generic noun instead: if you are writing about Japan's Ministry of Posts and Telecommunications, the way to avoid being repetitive and clunky isn't necessarily to use *MPT;* try *the ministry.*

One last caveat, from Steve G. Steinberg: "When it comes to technology, the greater the number of acronyms, the higher the bullshit factor. Developers trying to make things sound official end up using lots of obscure ones. Distributed object technology, with its endless lists—ORB, OLE, SOM, IDL—is a perfect example. Like postmodern lit theory, it creates a hermetic vocabulary so incomprehensible to outsiders that no one dares challenge it."

How do you style acronyms that morph into verbs?

A number of odd gerunds are growing out of new technologies and online experiences. Our style is to keep them as simple as possible, eschewing unnecessary apostrophes and doubling consonants in acronyms as we would in words:

CCing
HTMLing
IDing
MUDding

For past participles, use a contraction rather than -ed:

CC'd
HTML'd
ID'd

Make an exception for **MUDded**.

How do I style computer keys or onscreen buttons?

Computer keys referred to in text should be styled roman with initial caps, to underscore that the words refer to the names of functions. A story of a visit to The Computer Museum in Boston yielded this sentence: "Sam plays a Breakout-like arcade game onscreen: he capers on the keys, starting at Enter and shooting at a dead run to Caps Lock, launching himself off the keyboard and into a crashing encounter with the industrial carpet beyond."

Onscreen commands—point-and-click buttons, pulldown menus, or keystrokes—should be styled roman with initial caps: *Select Print in WordPerfect's button bar* or *Click on Open and type in the URL.*

Hyphens can help keep complex commands coherent: Control-Shift-F, Alt-Delete, Option-N.

Can you give me any help on using hyphens?

Let's forget about the most common use of hyphens in writing: to break a word by syllables at the end of a typed line. All you need for that is a good dictionary. (BTW, we use *Merriam Webster's Collegiate Dictionary*, Tenth Edition.)

It's all the new, weird compounds that we fret over. Our rules of thumb:

› Avoid hyphens for compound nouns, keeping a two-word noun open (*Web site*) or closing it up altogether (*homepage*). When in doubt, close it up. Since language evolves in one predictable direction—compounds start out as two words, then become hyphenated, then become solid—it's OK to leapfrog the middle step.

› Use hyphens in compound adjectives to distinguish between the modifier and the noun:

high-speed computer
56-kilobit-per-second modem
light-emitting diode

Except with compound modifiers consisting of an adverb ending in ly:

widely distributed mailing list
highly inflammatory post

› Some compound nouns are so prevalent in the digital world that they do not need to be hyphenated for clarity:

cable modem	[cable modem network)
cable TV	[cable TV show)
key escrow	[key escrow encryption)
open source	[open source software)
science fiction	[science fiction novel)
venture capital	[venture capital firm)

› Use double hyphens for triple compounds:

shoot-'em-up genre
cut-and-paste editing
ultra-high-density chips
pre-computer-age study

- Use hyphens when an adverb (or any other type of word, for that matter) combines with a participle to act as an adjective:

  well-known hacker
  much-despised copy editor
  interrupt-driven day

- However, when the adverb-participle combination follows a linking verb or form of "to be," the compound is then technically acting as a verb, not as an adjective, and so should not be hyphenated: *He is often derided in the Teen Chat forum* or *She is well respected in the Valley*.

- Don't be afraid of hyphens in two-noun compounds when the compound is modified by another word. The hyphen here distinguishes the adjective from the noun:

  new cable-modem
  cyber pipe-dream

- Use a hyphen when a prefix is combined with a proper noun:

  neo-Luddite
  anti-American
  non-Macintosh

Is PIN number redundant?

Yup. PIN stands for **personal identification number**. Put it in a ballooning class of digital redundancies, most of them born of acronyms:

CD-ROM disc
CISC computer
Cobol language
DSL line
DOS operating system
ISP provider
LCD display

PCS service
RAM memory
TCP/IP protocol

Our all-time favorite might be this malapropism uttered by Senator Alfonse D'Amato: "electronic email."

Saw the term *lossy compression*—is that just lousy spelling?

No, no, no. Lossy compression is a method of digital compression, a way to store files in fewer bytes. And more than once, *Wired* copy editors have been caught changing lossy to lousy. Ouch!

Index

Constance Hale established *Wired* magazine's house style and has been called "Marian the Librarian on a Harley," or "E. B. White on acid." With a master's degree in journalism from the University of California, Berkeley, she teaches writing and lives in Oakland, California. Fellow word maven Jessie Scanlon, an editor at *Wired*, has written for *I.D.* and *Interview* and lives in San Francisco.